Recruiting and Retaining

Generation Y

Teachers

*I dedicate this book to my grandchildren, Henry Rebore
and the twins, Tessa and Max Hamel, who along with my other
grandchildren have given new and wonderful meaning and purpose to my life.*

—Ronald W. Rebore

*I dedicate this book to the extended "Evans" family members
who live their lives, and enhance mine, with compassion, love, and fun.*

—Angela L. E. Walmsley

Recruiting and Retaining

Generation Y Teachers

Ronald W. Rebore ∘ Angela L. E. Walmsley

CORWIN
A SAGE Company

For information:

Corwin
A SAGE Company
2455 Teller Road
Thousand Oaks, California 91320
(800) 233-9936
Fax: (800) 417-2466
www.corwinpress.com

SAGE India Pvt. Ltd.
B 1/I 1 Mohan Cooperative
 Industrial Area
Mathura Road, New Delhi 110 044
India

SAGE Ltd.
1 Oliver's Yard
55 City Road
London EC1Y 1SP
United Kingdom

SAGE Asia-Pacific Pte. Ltd.
33 Pekin Street #02-01
Far East Square
Singapore 048763

Printed in the United States of America

Library of Congress Cataloging-in-Publication Data

Rebore, Ronald W.
Recruiting and retaining generation Y teachers/Ronald W. Rebore, Angela L. E. Walmsley.
    p. cm.
Includes bibliographical references and index.
ISBN 978-1-4129-6990-1 (cloth)
ISBN 978-1-4129-6991-8 (pbk.)
    1. Teachers—Recruiting—United States. 2. Teachers—Selection and appointment—United States. 3. Generation Y—Employment—United States. I. Walmsley, Angela Lynn Evans. II. Title.

LB2835.25.R42 2010
371.7'61371100973—dc22   2009019908

This book is printed on acid-free paper.

09 10 11 12 13 10 9 8 7 6 5 4 3 2 1

Acquisitions Editor:	Arnis Burvikovs
Associate Editor:	Desirée A. Bartlett
Production Editor:	Amy Schroller
Copy Editor:	Gretchen Treadwell
Typesetter:	C&M Digitals (P) Ltd.
Proofreader:	Charlotte Waisner
Cover Designer:	Scott Van Atta

Contents

Preface

Hiring new teachers is a common responsibility for all educational leaders. They will be constantly reviewing applicants for either internal moves or new hires. "New hires" may be veteran teachers moving into the district, or they may be adults who worked in another field and were trained later in life for teaching; however, most often, "new hires" are beginning teachers from the range of ages 21 to 25. In order to cultivate a positive learning environment, an educational leader must focus on "hiring for mission." Every school has its own culture and each "new hire" must be capable of thriving and succeeding in this culture. Also, administrators must always hire the best person—regardless of generation. This book is aimed at providing administrators with information about hiring teachers from Generation Y to help effectively integrate new teachers from this generation; however, it is important that administrators realize that the best teacher for a particular job could come from any generation.

The bulk of the new generation of teachers comes from what is known as Generation Y, or the Millennials. While there is no definitive agreement on a name or which years encompass Generation Y, it is generally believed that beginning teachers now, and for the next 10 to 15 years, are part of this generation. Generally speaking, these are the children born in the 1980s and 1990s to Baby Boomer parents. Because these children were the first to grow up in a society saturated with electronic technology, their needs and wants differ from those of previous teachers. They can be considered the first ultra-technological generation. In addition, other factors have significantly influenced this group, including changes in societal attitudes toward race and gender and the shifts in attitudes toward employer-employee relationships.

The purpose for writing this book was to explore the issue of hiring within the context of educational leadership and to provide practicing superintendents, principals, and other administrators with an understanding of the new generation of teachers. In addition, the authors provide a framework for hiring for mission and welcoming new teachers to a specific learning community. Also included in this framework is research about the expectations of this generation concerning diversity, technology, and enculturation. The authors will address the differences in communication that this generation expects and how to communicate effectively between past and present generations of teachers. At the end, a glossary of terms and a list of suggested reading, organized by each chapter, are provided.

Acknowledgments

We thank Rachel Mirecki, a graduate assistant at Saint Louis University, for her time in proofreading the manuscript, and for the addition of information regarding Generation Y and technology.

Corwin gratefully acknowledges the contributions of the following individuals:

Nancy Betler, NBCT, Instructional Specialist
National Academic League Commissioner
Charlotte, NC

Becki Cohn-Vargas, Director
Elementary Education and Staff Development
El Sobrante, CA

Linda C. Diaz, Teacher on Special Assignment
Monroe County School District
Key West, FL

Susan Hudson, President
School Improvement Services
Nashville, TN

Steve Hutton, Educational Consultant
Villa Hills, KY

Michael Ingrisani, Dean of Faculty
The Browning School
New York, NY

About the Authors

Ronald W. Rebore, Sr., PhD, is a professor at Saint Louis University located in Saint Louis, Missouri. His professional experience includes twenty-two years as an administrator: nine years as an assistant superintendent of a medium-sized suburban school district, five years as the superintendent of schools in a small suburban school district, and eight years as the superintendent of schools for a large metropolitan school district employing approximately four thousand staff members with an annual budget of approximately 170 million dollars.

Rebore has a Bachelor of Arts degree in Philosophy, a Master of Education degree in Counseling and Guidance, and a Doctor of Philosophy degree in Educational Leadership. He has taught graduate level courses in educational leadership for approximately twenty-two years including ethics courses. Rebore has over forty publications, twelve of which are books. Two of the books have been published in multiple editions. The ninth edition of *Human Resources Administration in Education: A Management Approach* will be released in 2009. Two of his books have been translated into Chinese and have been adopted for use in preparing educational administrators in China.

Angela L. E. Walmsley, PhD, is an associate professor at Saint Louis University located in Saint Louis, Missouri. She has been working in the field of education for approximately fifteen years. In that time, she has taught middle school and high school mathematics both in the United States and the United Kingdom; she has taught introductory education courses, graduate-level advanced education and mathematics education courses at two universities in the Saint Louis area, and she is currently teaching statistical and educational research courses at Saint Louis University.

Walmsley has a joint Bachelor of Science degree in Mathematics and Teaching from the University of Illinois at Urbana-Champaign, a Master in Education degree in Mathematics Education and a Diploma in Statistics from the University of Dublin: Trinity College in Dublin, Ireland; and a Doctor of Philosophy degree in Curriculum and Instruction with an emphasis on Mathematics Education and Educational Research from Saint Louis University. In addition, she holds teaching certificates for the states of Illinois and Missouri, as well as Northern Ireland in the United Kingdom.

1

Characteristics of the New Generation of Teachers

CHAPTER OBJECTIVES

- To introduce Generation Y
- To describe the issues surrounding vacancies in the classroom
- To describe the various types of teachers entering these classrooms
- To describe the characteristics of Generation Y
- To describe multiple intelligences and emotional intelligence and connect them to Generation Y teachers

VIGNETTE

Andy is a Generation Y teacher who has just taken a job in a local school district. During his interview, he was particularly disturbed by one of the questions posed: "How long do you expect to remain a teacher at this school?" He explained that he chose teaching as a career for life, and hoped that his skills and the fit in this particular school would enable him to be a lifelong teacher there. He then proceeded to ask why the question was posed, wondering if there was a high teacher turnover. The interviewer explained that of all

> *Generation Y teachers they had hired in the last five years, approximately 75 percent left within three years. The turnover was becoming a huge problem for the school as it was creating instability among the staff, students, and parents. The principal, in particular, was worried about how this was affecting morale in the school and the school culture, never mind the intense cost and time for hiring every year.*
>
> *After Andy started his job, he approached the principal again about this constant issue of turnover. He suggested that they meet to establish what might be working or not working for these new teachers. During the course of the year, Andy and the principal established, among other things, a more modern mentoring program, some professional development opportunity choices for newer teachers, and some guidelines for acceptable technological use within the school. Andy explained that as a Generation Y teacher, he expected all these things to be established in his new position. He was glad to help the principal start to evaluate some of the criteria by which Generation Y teachers may be judging the school or district, and to think about changes that would help integrate new teachers to the school.*

CHARACTERISTICS OF GENERATION Y

Of course, as is the situation with all prior and future generations, each has a unique set of characteristics. Thus Generation Y teachers, assistant principals, principals, and other administrators are somewhat culturally different from other generations. These differences are generalizations and may not apply to a given person. Also, some Generation Y people may exhibit only a few of the indicators. The purpose for including these differences here and in the five subsequent chapters is to inform and assist principals and superintendents as they hire and integrate Generation Y employees with other generations of employees. The characteristics are in no specific order of importance or relevance.

One of the most important characteristics of Generation Y is the desire to trust authority. Baby Boomers traditionally had little trust or admiration for authority and government. What Generation Y employees want from their leaders are examples of behaviors that can be admired, leading toward trust for those leaders. It's difficult to ask people to trust principals and superintendents just on blind faith supported merely by the title of their leadership position. Admired behavior is a powerful force that can transform a school or school district into a true learning community where all employees feel appreciated and know that they can count on the goodness of intention when administrators make decisions that can affect their lives.

Another characteristic of Generation Y has been reflected even in the popular media in tandem with the economic crisis facing the United States and, indeed, all world markets. For some time, people have placed a significant amount of social and economic self-worth on what they owned in terms of property and investment portfolios. However, now there is a shift that economists refer to as human capital. It is the value one places on making a living, which is based on an individual's work ethic, skills, and education. How these human assets are utilized in getting a job constitutes a kind of capital that will not be easily diminished. Of course, there are fewer jobs, but the competition for the remaining jobs will be fierce and the winners will probably be those with the most human capital. This is the way that Generation Y looks upon their future economic stability. They value salary and fringe benefits along with wanting to get ahead in a shorter period of time as they seek out purposeful employment (Kiviat, 2009).

VACANCIES IN THE CLASSROOM

In 2001, the government projected that over 2 million new teachers for the classroom would need to be hired in that decade (Teachers, 2001). According to the National Center for Education Statistics (as cited in Marvel, Lyter, Peltola, Strizek, & Morton, 2006), the average turnover rate is 17 percent a year. The National Education Association (as cited in Kopkowski, 2007) states that one-third of teachers leave within the first three years and up to 46 percent leave in the first five years. Issues leading to vacancies in the classroom include retirement, career shifts, personal problems, salary, lack of funding, lack of respect and support from parents and/or administrators, lack of adequate time for professional growth and planning, and bureaucratic initiatives such as the No Child Left Behind Act. More specifically, vacancies in the classroom can be categorized three ways: teachers leave the classroom because of retirement, teachers leave the classroom for personal reasons or to change careers, and teachers transfer schools. No matter what the reason, it is obvious that continual vacancies occur in America's classrooms at a significantly high rate.

Constant teacher turnover costs America hundreds of millions of dollars annually to recruit and prepare teachers (Futernick, 2007, p. 1); thus, it is crucial that administrators arm themselves with knowledge about hiring and retaining the best teachers possible. Other "costs" that are affiliated include the loss of teacher experience related to instructional continuity and appropriate behaviors. It is unlikely that teacher attrition and turnover rates will decrease dramatically over the next five to ten years; thus, to increase stability in the school, administrators should have the tools and knowledge to hire staff as effectively as possible. This requires understanding why vacancies occur in their schools or districts, and what types of teachers are expected to replace these vacancies.

NEWLY HIRED VETERAN TEACHERS

Many teachers who are hired in a school or district are actually experienced, "veteran" teachers who change districts because of spousal moves, opportunities for safer working conditions, better pay, and/or changes in what may appear to be a stagnant school. Hiring veteran teachers is very different than hiring new teachers because the individuals already have so much knowledge and experience about education. Because of this, they often "cost more" than newly qualified teachers. Many progressive districts hire veteran teachers because they have a strong "track record." However, their experiences may be in a very different type of school; therefore, it is crucial that the hiring administrator be satisfied that the teacher will fit with the mission and culture of the school (this is discussed further in Chapter 3). Nevertheless, veteran teachers can be a great asset to any school because they typically need less mentoring and coaching and can be extremely effective from the beginning.

PROFESSIONALS CHANGING CAREERS TO TEACHING

Another type of new teacher is one who changes a current career to teaching. Sometimes these individuals complete a traditional teaching bachelor's degree, essentially "going back to school" from one career to teaching. However, one of the major recent trends in education has been alternative certification. For example, in order to meet the demand for qualified teachers in positions that are difficult to fill, such as mathematics and science, some state departments of education have developed alternative certification programs. Such programs usually require the interested person to have a college or university degree along with related experience. The purpose is to provide a way for qualified individuals to obtain certification in a relatively short period of time. Such programs are usually offered through colleges and universities. The curriculum varies while the emphasis is placed on teaching methodologies, along with necessary instruction in child and adolescent development. For example, a retired chemical engineer may seek such certification in order to teach high school chemistry. The target population is people seeking a second career.

Alternative certification as a means to enter the classroom can also include a holding a bachelor's degree in a particular field, and then completing teacher certification or a master's degree with certification in teaching; completing a bachelor's teaching degree while being employed in schools; and completing a program such as Teach for America or Troops to Teachers.

Despite the popularity of alternative certification and adults returning to enter the teaching profession, the vast majority of newly certified teachers are traditional-age graduates from a four-year university program. These new teachers are Generation Y.

THE EMERGENCE OF GENERATION Y

While no exact definition of Generation Y exists, many agree that it is the generation of children born approximately between 1980 and 1995. Some sources say Generation Y are those born between 1977 and 1986; others say between 1976 and 2000; and still others say 1977 and 1995. This places the first of Generation Y college students having attended college around the year 2000. This generation is preceded by Generation X, and many Generation Y children are children of the Baby Boomer generation. Along with being the most diverse group of individuals to enter the teaching field, some characteristics of this generation that will be discussed more in detail are their tendencies to:

- Communicate more through technology than in person
- Value benefits at work
- Seek career advancement, desire flexibility and higher pay
- Work in teams and possess high energy
- Work hard but also enjoy pleasure
- Be financially savvy
- Want constant feedback
- Work among and with a diverse group of individuals
- Multitask proficiently
- Like change

Some of the issues related to Generation Y's upbringing include hovering and very involved parents, being nurtured, being programmed with lots of activities, and being taught that they have high worth. At this writing, they are the most child-centered generation. Sometimes they are described as high maintenance but also high performance. They are also known as the Nexters, Millennials, iGen, or the Internet (or Net) generation.

Many Generation Y teachers were recently Generation Y students who were deeply connected to their parents. Many relied on e-mail and cell phones to communicate daily with their parents—especially as they attended college elsewhere (Tapscott, 1998, p. 23). They also make decisions jointly with their parents who are often quite demanding (Howe & Strauss, 2007, p. 4). They emerged as a group of young adults who like collaboration and working with others. Diversity is a part of their lives, much like technology, and in using technology (where ethnicity and gender are often invisible), they learn to work well together. They also spend a lot of money. Most Generation Y high school and college students have credit cards with fairly high limits. Companies market quite a lot to this age group, as there are so many Millennials with much spending power (Pletka, 2007, p. 35).

As can be seen by the lists generated above, there are many characteristics to cover about Generation Y. Probably the starkest difference between Generation Y and any other generation is the large, available access to information. All traditional college-age graduates entering schools as teachers this year are from Generation Y. These people believe that knowledge is power, and all knowledge can be found quickly through the Internet (Wong & Wong, n.d.). This group of individuals is particularly technology savvy. They blog, Google, and use Wikipedia to acquire sources of information.

Howe and Strauss (2007) believe that this new generation of graduating students will enter the workforce making changes as the Baby Boomer generation did during the 1960s (p. 4). The young adults entering professions today are very ethnically diverse as well as dominated by females. They are typically eager to please others and work hard to achieve their goals in the process. Along with enjoying group work and community service (Levine & Cureton, 1998, p. 4), they enjoy their families, expecting to live at home or near their parents as they enter the workforce. With all of these characteristics in mind, Howe and Strauss (2007) believe that there are seven core traits that can be identified for Generation Y:

1. They are made to feel they are *special*.

2. They have been *sheltered* by their parents and society.

3. They are *confident* with high levels of trust and optimism.

4. They have developed strong team building skills (*team-oriented*).

5. They are *conventional*, following rules and standards.

6. They have been *pressured* to study hard and excel.

7. They are high *achieving* and highly educated.

As stated earlier, another important aspect of Generation Y is the diversity of the group. Not only have they lived with diversity their whole lives, the racial and ethnic makeup of the group is more different than ever before. "In 1999, nonwhites and Latinos accounted for nearly 36 percent of the eighteen-or-under population, a share half-again higher than for the Boomer age brackets, and nearly *three times* higher than for today's seniors" (Howe & Strauss, 2000, p. 15). Howe and Strauss (2000) also state that one in five has an immigrant parent, and one in ten has a noncitizen parent—making this generation very globally minded and connected.

The characteristics described here provide some background knowledge about differences between Generation Y and previous generations. While more topics will be discussed at length in the proceeding chapters, there are two important issues that need to be addressed in this chapter for further understanding about Generation Y, multiple intelligences and emotional intelligence.

MULTIPLE INTELLIGENCES

Generation Y has been the most child-centered generation to attend school. Coinciding with this, schools have changed to include diverse learners in an attempt to create educated and successful young adults. The theory of multiple intelligences has facilitated this movement for Generation Y. The multiple intelligences theory was first proposed by Howard Gardner in

1983, and has received much recognition since (Dvinicki, 2004, pp. 214–215). This theory states that it is incorrect to assume that there is only one type of intelligence, such as IQ; instead, there are multiple types of intelligences. The seven original intelligences in this theory are (1) visual-spatial, (2) linguistic, (3) logical-mathematical, (4) bodily-kinesthetic, (5) musical-rhythmic, (6) interpersonal-social, and (7) intrapersonal-introspective. Two others have followed, identified as naturalist-physical world and existential intelligences (Fogarty & Stoehr, 2008, p. 6). It is possible to excel in more than one intelligence, but probably not all. Because students learn in different ways and have talents in various things at various levels, an effective school is one that can create the most conducive learning environment for children despite their learning differences. Therefore, students should be immersed in multiple methods of learning to best understand the curriculum.

Gardner believes that there are "multiple approaches to understanding" in the following six ways to approach topics: (1) narrative (telling stories), (2) numerical (using numbers or statistics), (3) existential (couched in philosophy), (4) aesthetic (using art), (5) hands-on (using activities), and (6) social (using group methods). The real point of practicality with the theory of multiple intelligences is that teachers and administrators must realize that there are multiple ways that people learn best, and using a variety of techniques reaches the greatest number of students. For example, a history teacher might use a film (narrative) as well as a group discussion project (social) for a particular topic. Using a variety of techniques helps to focus on the process of learning and not the differences among learners.

Generation Y teachers may have been taught themselves as children in schools or classrooms with teachers knowing and planning lessons around the theory of multiple intelligences. This enables an administrator to ask these teachers to utilize various intelligences in their own teaching, and to help facilitate older teachers' methods if needed. Administrators should expect teachers to allow children the freedom to learn content through a variety of techniques. Using multiple methods for teaching and learning allows children to utilize their strengths in understanding regardless of the school's curriculum goals.

In particular, Gardner explains that interpersonal intelligence and intrapersonal intelligence deal with individuals' abilities to understand other people and themselves, respectively. These intelligences were precursors to the theory of emotional intelligence—another important aspect for all teachers and schools.

EMOTIONAL INTELLIGENCE

Emotional intelligence has been described by Goleman (1995) as a trait whereby individuals must develop an understanding of themselves and others both emotionally and intellectually; then they can direct inter-actions and activities with others successfully (Fink, 2003, p. 47). Descriptors for emotional intelligence include being able to motivate oneself when faced with frustrations, to control one's impulses, to delay gratification as appropriate, to regulate one's moods as it pertains to interactions with others, and to empathize and hope (Goleman, 1995, p. 34). In other words, emotional intelligence relates to interpersonal skills—those who manage feelings well and deal effectively with others' feelings. This is crucial in school communication and interactions. All teachers must "read" students, parents, and administrators' body lan-guage, interpret the feeling behind statements made, and interact on a regular basis. In addition, personal intelligences in schools must be taught to children; in order to do so, teachers must understand emotional intelligence.

Often, the most successful people in life are not those who have the highest GPA or IQ, but instead are those who can communicate and interact positively with others within socially acceptable boundaries. Teachers of all generations typically must have positive emotional intel-ligence in order to be effective in the classroom and within a school. There has been concern that Generation Y teachers do not understand social boundaries and lack emotional intelligence due to their experi-ences of dealing in virtual social networks rather than in reality-based social interactions including face to face interactions. Walmsley and McManemy (2008) have coined the term, "character dysfunction," (par. 3) to describe the lack of social skills affecting one's ability to create and maintain successful professional relationships. Teachers with character dysfunctions cannot be as effective with others on a regular basis because they lack social abilities. For example, suppose a teacher cannot look directly at fellow teachers or parents while discussing children or a par-ticular problem in school, or, a teacher quickly "flies off the handle" when a fellow teacher suggests a different approach to a discipline prob-lem. These are simple examples of individuals who need education and practice regarding socially appropriate and acceptable behavior in a pro-fessional context. While technology can be "blamed" for the lack of inter-personal skills, it is not a valid excuse. Many teachers who use technology on a regular basis are able to have positive social interactions. And, while teachers of all ages may lack positive social skills, an administrator should be aware that the issue of emotional intelligence may need to be addressed more with newly hired teachers.

Some educators group emotional intelligence and character education together. Administrators can use character education as a tool for educat-ing students, but also as reminders of how they expect teachers to interact in positive ways. Strong emotional intelligence between administrator and teacher breeds a positive school culture (school culture is addressed in

Chapter 3). Can emotional intelligence be taught? Goleman (1995) provides one theory in understanding and teaching emotional intelligence following these steps: know one's own emotions; manage one's own emotions; motivate oneself; recognize emotions in others; and handle relationships with others by managing others' emotions (p. 43). Children need to be taught emotional intelligence in schools because it will promote the social interactions and welfare of all children. Promotion of emotional intelligence can educate students in social competence and prevention of behavioral problems; this creates strong relationship-building skills and empathy among children.

The importance of emotional intelligence and how it relates to the success of an individual has been debated. However, Mayer (2001) states that emotional intelligence and academic intelligence should be equally examined, as true success could be a solid partnership between the two (p. 24). In fact, Elias, Hunter, and Kress (2001) state, "When we look closer at 'academics,' we can see further similarities of curriculum content areas and EI [emotional intelligence] and see that EI skills rest clearly within the central mission of the schools" (pp. 139–140). Therefore, administrators must be aware and articulate the expectation of their teachers to effectively teach skills related to interactions and relationships alongside academics.

SUMMARY

Vacancies in the classroom are being filled with various types of teachers. This includes veteran teachers moving areas or returning to the classroom as well as professionals changing careers. However, the majority of newly entering teachers are those from traditional education programs who are around age 22. These teachers are from the latest generation of adults entering the workforce: Generation Y. There are unique characteristics defining this generation as they enter and fill positions in the workforce. Finally, the issues of multiple intelligences and emotional intelligence are equally pertinent to teaching children and interacting with Generation Y teachers.

CASE STUDY A

Mrs. Mallioux has recently moved to a rural area and has taken a job as principal of the local high school. Upon arrival, she realizes that she needs to fill five teacher vacancies. As the school year begins, she collects data on demographics of her teachers. She realizes the majority of teachers have been in the building for over ten years, and now she has five new teachers. Upon further investigation, she realizes that the newest teachers have continually left the building and district over the past five years, with most of them only staying one year to teach. Since she is interested in having a diverse group of teachers of all ages, she decides she must inquire as to why so many of the newer teachers have been leaving. In particular, she wants to build a strong teaching staff with minimal turnover as she begins her own administration career in this district.

She decides to interview veteran teachers in the building to assess their opinions regarding newly hired teachers. She also gains permission from her five new teachers (all whom have just graduated from college and are entering their first teaching job) to watch them closely and to meet regularly with them to fully understand issues they face. From her research and what she saw at her last school where she was a teacher, Mrs. Mallioux notices that beginning teachers often feel a lack of collaboration and solidarity in the profession. In particular, new teachers often seek each other out as a support network. While this type of support is helpful, other novice teachers may not have the experience and knowledge to offer suggestions and advice that the veteran teachers may be able to provide. In other words, these new teachers are expected to be experts from the beginning. The stress and unrealistic expectations lead many young teachers to leave.

Aware of this information and the school's history of new teacher attrition, Mrs. Mallioux decides she is going to focus on a mentoring program partnering veteran teachers with her five new teachers. When she approaches the ten veteran teachers about becoming strong mentors for these new teachers, she learns that they are not necessarily interested. Some of their comments are, "Why do we need to put our time and effort into mentoring? They all leave anyway." "Those new teachers use so many different teaching methods and styles and I can't help them." And, "I can't stand all that flashy technology they have . . . they would rather 'Google' it than listen to what I have to say."

Analyze the scenario described above by answering the following questions:

- How should Mrs. Mallioux proceed?
- What other programs or meetings can she have with the veteran teachers to begin a mentoring program?
- What other programs or meetings can she have with the new teachers to understand their generation and needs?
- What interactions between the new and veteran teachers should Mrs. Mallioux facilitate, and how?
- Mrs. Mallioux is worried that the new teachers are leaving because of some of the characteristics she has heard about their generation. Provide some examples of those characteristics that might be interpreted negatively by the veteran teachers.

CASE STUDY B

Over the years, Dr. Young has worked to build a strong school district. He became superintendent of a small urban school system five years ago, and he has worked tirelessly at providing teacher in-service, family information sessions, monetary allocations for teachers to further their education, and strategies to improve students' test scores. In particular, he has focused his district on revising curriculum to make a strong, cohesive plan for all academic content areas from elementary through high school. Dr. Young feels that academically, his district is doing great. His next plan for strengthening the schools in his district is to begin focusing on the issue of emotional intelligence and character education; however, he is worried that his academic strength will weaken if he begins to focus on emotional intelligence.

Dr. Young asks for five teachers, one from each school building, to volunteer to be part of a task force to provide him with some information on emotional intelligence and how it can be used not only in the schools, but in the curriculum where it does not diminish the focus on academics. He is also interested in teachers' perceptions about focusing the district on emotional intelligence. After two months, this group reports to Dr. Young. Some of the information includes teachers' perceptions that students do need some sort of character education, in particular at the elementary school level; teachers' perceptions that the brightest students are not always the most successful as they leave high school and move on in their careers; and teachers' perceptions that students should learn more in school than just academics. Regarding how emotional intelligence is currently or could be included in the curriculum, some examples the teachers developed are:

- In analyzing literature, students are expected to understand feelings and motivations of characters (Elias et al., 2001, p. 140).
- In studying history, students should understand motives behind a chronology of events.
- In learning to read and write, children often "free write" about their experiences. This almost always includes feelings and opinions as they begin to develop essays and stories.

After Dr. Young receives the feedback, he decides to pursue the initiative of incorporating emotional intelligence in his district.

Analyze the scenario described above by answering the following questions:

- What should be Dr. Young's first step in implementing an emotional intelligence component into the curriculum?
- In your opinion, at which level is it most important to focus on emotional intelligence: elementary, middle, or high school?
- List at least three other ways that emotional intelligence can be incorporated into academics at your school or in your district.

- Do you agree that the teachers' perceptions about the need for emotional intelligence are representative of needs in many American schools?
- Provide a situation you have seen or been a part of in your building where a teacher did not have strong interpersonal skills or lacked emotional intelligence.
- How could you explain to parents the need for an emotional intelligence aspect to the curriculum?
- Do you agree that emotional intelligence and interpersonal skills are equally as important as academic ability? Explain why or why not.
- In what ways, if any, have you seen Generation Y adults lack emotional intelligence?

EXERCISE

Do you know the accurate characteristics for Generation Y?

Below are general statements about Generation Y. List T (true) or F (false) next to each statement. (Answers are at the bottom of the quiz.) Some statements will be controversial; you may list undecided as long as you can support your choice.

_____ 1. Generation Y adults have never witnessed severe economic trouble.

_____ 2. Collaborative learning is second-nature to Generation Y teachers.

_____ 3. Generation Y teachers feel generally negative about themselves and their working abilities.

_____ 4. Generation Y is the least prejudiced generation about race.

_____ 5. Generation Y professionals do not feel they can talk easily about religion and faith.

_____ 6. Work-life balance is important to Generation Y workers.

_____ 7. Generation Y workers are generally not self initiated risk-takers.

_____ 8. Generation Y would rather be "supervised" than "coached."

_____ 9. Generation Y and Generation X have similar technological skills and needs.

_____ 10. Generation Y expects diversity and up-to-date technology in the workplace.

Answers: 1.F, 2.T, 3.F, 4.T, 5.F, 6.T, 7.T, 8.F, 9.F, 10.T

CHAPTER FOCUS QUESTIONS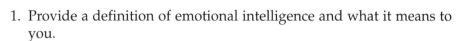

1. Provide a definition of emotional intelligence and what it means to you.

2. Provide some examples of how emotional intelligence can be infused in your school's academic curriculum.

3. How have Generation Y teachers in your school or district used multiple intelligences to enhance instruction?

4. What characteristics of Generation Y have you seen in your recently hired teachers?

5. What are the most common reasons for vacancies in the classroom?

6. Can you identify and explain any differences in relationship building among Generation Y teachers because of the different relationships these teachers may have had with their own parents during their upbringing?

2

Marketing and Recruiting Generation Y Teachers, Staff Members, and Administrators

---

CHAPTER OBJECTIVES

- To explain why marketing and recruiting activities need to be tailored specifically to Generation Y applicants for teaching, staff, and administrative positions
- To identify the variables that affect the marketing and recruitment of Generation Y teachers, staff members, and administrators
- To explore the methods of marketing and recruitment that would be most effective in attracting Generation Y teachers, staff members, and administrators

Vignette

Mrs. Chaudhury is a teacher who has recently been appointed as an interim principal of a high school in a suburban school district. She has served as a history teacher in the school for the last ten years. Upon her appointment as interim principal, she realizes that one of her first priorities is to hire three new teachers for the upcoming school year. Because it has been so long since she applied as a teacher, she decides to begin her own research about advertising and hiring via the school and school district Web sites.

As she begins her exploration, she is troubled by what she can and cannot find. First, the school's mission is hidden in the Web site, very difficult to locate. There are lots of pictures of students and teachers in the building, but these are not provided with any context. Also, there is no central page describing the hiring process or containing forms to be completed. When she looks through her school's Web site, she realizes that an "outsider," that is, someone who is either not an employee, parent, or student in the school district, would have difficulty understanding the school culture and day-to-day operations or how to apply for a job.

In addition to not being able to find information, one of the most frustrating things Mrs. Chaudhury discovers is that old Web pages are not ever "taken down." Therefore, when an individual uses the school's search engine for a particular topic, old information easily surfaces. With her knowledge of Generation Y employees, she realizes that not having a manageable Web site for the school could be very problematic in recruiting potential employees. Further, one of the strategic planning goals of the school includes continued and appropriate use of technology in the classroom. Mrs. Chaudhury realizes that teachers who may specialize in the use of technology may be discouraged by the Web site and not consider a position at the school because of the appearance of a lack of support for technology. Therefore, Mrs. Chaudhury requests a meeting with the superintendent and the director of information technology for the district to see what can be done before she advertises the new positions.

CHARACTERISTICS OF GENERATION Y

Generation Y teachers and administrators want to be convinced, rather than informed, about the benefits of becoming an employee in a given school district. Thus principals, superintendents, and other administrators must use the various techniques employed by marketing firms to convince Generation Y teachers and administrators that accepting employment in a certain school district is a good opportunity. As a consequence of this characteristic, school districts need to conceptualize recruitment as marketing rather than advertising (Lubman, 1993; Rebore, 2007).

Research by Half (2008) indicates that Generation Y teachers and administrators want their work experience to be enjoyable, but also accept that it will be demanding and challenging. Further, Generation Y teachers and administrators look upon their work experience more in the vein of a career or vocation and definitely do not consider it as just a job. This perspective is important because they see themselves doing something that is worthwhile, that has value to themselves, others, and society in general (Lubman, 1993; Rebore, 2007).

Generation Y is also different from other current generations in the degree to which they develop their career paths. At some point in their careers, prior generations of teachers and administrators come to a decision in their professional experience concerning what they want to accomplish, usually in a linear fashion, throughout the rest of their careers. For example, a teacher might decide to become an assistant principal and may leave his present teaching position to obtain that desired position in another school district. In order to prepare for this career, he might decide to obtain a master's degree in school administration. Generation Y teachers and administrators tend to be more focused on balancing the demands of their professional and personal life experiences while maintaining upward mobility. If and when that sense of balance diminishes, they then search for alternative positions that could provide the personal fulfillment that they have lost. It is an inward search rather than a strict career path that propels Generation Y (Lubman, 1993; Rebore, 2007).

Thus the same inner passion also affects Generation Y administrators who might be searching for superintendent's positions. Of course, Generation Y teachers and administrators searching for personal fulfillment will certainly come to realize that, like their counterpartners, they must also obtain the credentials of master's degrees and/or a doctorate in school leadership or administration in order to make themselves available to new opportunities. In this respect, Generation Y wants to achieve the next level of professional responsibilities much quicker than prior generations. It is fair to state that teachers from Generation Y want to work in a school district that provides opportunities for both professional and personal growth (Lubman, 1993; Rebore, 2007).

Other research points out that Generation Y teachers and administrators are also searching for security and stability in the work experience (Coomes & DeBard, 2004). Thus they are looking for a school districts that are financially solvent and, if not growing in population, then at least stable.

It is interesting to note that approximately 25 percent of Generation Y consult their parents or others before accepting a position. Another implication for recruiting Generation Y teachers and administrators is the extensive use they make of school districts' Web sites in order to gather information about the district, which will ultimately influence their decisions to search for positions in the district that meet their needs and desires. In general, approximately 75 percent of Generation Y will study the Web site of the company or school district that they are interested in (Lubman, 1993; Rebore, 2007).

GENERATION Y APPLICANTS

Although the focus of human resources administration is on how to carry out the activities and practices that will result in the hiring and retaining of qualified teachers, staff members, and administrators, the emergence of the present generation of applicants requires very specific changes in the marketing and recruiting processes. In other words, it is important to understand the factors that influence the career choices of prospective Generation Y candidates.

Because people have different skills and personalities, the strategies that are developed to market and recruit employees must always be focused on the current culture of the times. However, Generation Y appears to be much more different than other generations in terms of what attracts them to specific schools and school districts. Overall, marketing and recruiting strategies must take into account the fact that ability, interest, and personality interface in a number of possible positions. For example, a successful high school language arts teacher may also be a good candidate for an administrative position in community relations, particularly in the publication of school district marketing materials. Both of these positions generally require the skills to communicate ideas in writing. Also, both would position the employee able to promote the vision and goals of the school district to parents and taxpayers in a human relations setting. Essentially, candidates for certain positions should not be limited to just those who already perform similar tasks.

It is also important to understand that people change over time in relation to their competencies and preferences. Of course, this occurs because time and experience have an effect on a person's perspective. Everyone makes career and personal adjustments to the changing times. Thus, it is unwise to assume that current employees are not interested in other positions within a school or school district that are different from their present situation. Consequently, internal searching is always a good strategy in identifying potential applicants for positions.

A fundamental principle in human resources administration is that employment satisfaction depends on the degree to which employees can utilize their skills that are supported by their interests and values. A school district that is experiencing a high degree of employee turnover in certain positions should evaluate the responsibilities of the position and the types of skills that are necessary to fulfill those responsibilities. Obviously, it is important to find the linkage between interest, values, and skills. For example, a superintendent in a metropolitan area with a very unionized faculty will need to possess the skills of compromise and a deep understanding of the value negotiating process, as well as an appreciation for the value of unions.

Naturally, employment choices are influenced by other considerations such as salary, fringe benefits, working conditions, and the opportunity for advancement. The juxtaposition of these considerations will vary depending on the individual. In marketing and recruitment activities, it is very important to inform candidates about these considerations so that they can make informed decisions about pursuing different positions. It happens more often than not that a person may be so intent on obtaining a position that they neglect to review considerations such as salary, fringe benefits, and working conditions until an offer is made, which may result in a refusal of the offer. At times, this search may cost the school district a considerable amount of money without obtaining tangible results.

It is not uncommon for applicants to accept positions in schools or school districts through internal processes by which they balance personal characteristics, such as interests and skills, with working conditions. The process of balancing compromises is predicated by applicants' abilities to conjure up how they will like the new position and the environment within which they will work. Happiness in working conditions is crucial to success in the position.

Assessment centers were developed because of the notion that every applicant and new hire will not like all the considerations that are present within a given school or school district. Assessment centers help employees determine if the career path that they are taking in a school district will continue to satisfy their needs and aspirations. This is particularly pertinent to Generation Y employees. For example, at an assessment center, Generation Y employees will have the opportunity to match up their interests, skills, and aspirations into a career path plan. For instance, a teacher may have aspirations to become a department chairperson or a director of curriculum in the future. The plan would allow this person to have various opportunities to intern in such situations that would help the teacher make future career decisions. This is a strategy for retaining good employees who would otherwise be seeking positions in other school districts. It is a way of retaining and rewarding excellent employees and recognizing that internal candidates who are already immersed in the school culture are often more suited for the position than an external candidate. Successful and satisfied employees are a good indicator of the quality and success of the marketing and recruitment processes.

Job success is the only true measure of how effective the marketing and recruitment process has been. This implication is often overlooked, and many school districts never evaluate their marketing and recruitment procedures through a follow-up study on the success of those who were hired.

THE MILIEU

While in some areas of the country there is not a shortage of teachers, generally there exists a shortage of qualified teachers. It is always true that there is a shortage of teachers in special education, mathematics, science, and English as a second language in certain school districts. Also, there is a shortage of both African American and Hispanic teachers and administrators.

Of course, the marketing and recruitment processes depend on the existence of colleges and universities with a school of education located in the not-too-distant vicinity of the school district. Location of the school is also important for obtaining the necessary labor pool for school bus drivers, cafeteria workers, and housekeeping personnel.

CONSIDERATIONS AFFECTING MARKETING AND RECRUITMENT

Diversity

In marketing and recruiting Generation Y employees, human resources administrators need to think about diversity as being much broader than just ethnicity. A hallmark of our nation is immigration. Historically, we are a nation of immigrants who came from both Eastern and Western Europe. While there is still a flow of immigrants from Eastern Europe, most immigrants come from Asia, the Americas, and other parts of the world. Within the next fifty years, the majority population in the United States will be of Hispanic decent. While the Caucasian population will continue to decrease, significant gains will also be made by Asians and other ethnic groups. In particular, there will continue to be an increase in mixed-race or biracial individuals. These changes will affect the United States not only ethnically but also religiously. Instead of being a nation of only Christians and Jews, the United States now has a considerable number of Muslims, Hindus, and Confucians. In fact, the United States is the most diverse nation in the world.

The issue of diversity is crucial for human resources administrators in relation to Generation Y because every school district needs to have teachers, staff members, and administrators who are somewhat ethnically the same as the children in the schools. Also, children need to experience teachers, staff members, and administrators who are representative of the larger population in the United States (Au & Blake, 2003, pp. 192–205). Thus, these are both immediate and long-term considerations that mandate the development of recruitment strategies (Fielder, 1993, pp. 33–34).

Some school districts make a practice of promoting already-hired Generation Y employees into administrative positions; therefore, a classroom Generation Y teacher may become a department chairperson. It is important for Generation Y employees to recognize that a school district provides them with opportunities to advance their careers through promotion to positions of greater responsibility. This situation will probably help Generation Y employees make long-term commitments to the districts. In like manner, Generation Y employees should also be made aware of the link between job performance and promotion. Human resources administrators should develop performance evaluation procedures that allow employees to demonstrate that they are capable of handling higher-level tasks. Of course, the performance evaluation process is the typical way for employees to document the quality of their performance.

Federal law concerning affirmative action and equal employment opportunity basically prohibits discrimination in marketing and recruitment because of race, age, disability, military service, color, religion, sex, pregnancy, and national origin. Internal promotion does not nullify affirmative action requirements. In fact, affirmative action and equal employment opportunity are important considerations in developing and implementing marketing and recruitment practices and procedures.

The Image of the School District

A second consideration in relation to marketing and recruitment is the image of the school district. Generation Y applicants are probably not interested in pursuing job opportunities in school districts that have a negative image in the professional community. For example, a district that is involved in a lawsuit filed by a former tenured teacher whose employment was terminated allegedly for inadequate performance might give applicants pause in pursuing employment. Further, the policies of the boards of education could be deterrents to potential applicants. For example, a district that places high expectations on teachers to raise student standardized test scores might not want to be placed in that type of situation, especially if the district lacks adequate curricular and instructional support. Administrative procedures and processes could also have a detrimental effect if, for example, they do not provide for procedural due process in the performance-evaluation processes for teachers.

Thus, the quality of the working situation becomes an important aspect of the decision-making process for Generation Y. The image of the school district becomes a prerequisite that could stymie all but the most desperate to consider applying for and accepting a position in such a school district.

The Position

The third consideration for marketing and recruitment is the requirement of the position. If the position is considered to be extremely challenging, but lacks a reasonable salary or the potential for promotion, Generation Y job seekers may pass over the job opportunity. For example, a high school drama-teaching position might be available due to the retirement of the former teacher who was very successful in the position. The retiring teacher directed a significant number of plays and the yearly musical. She had been with the school district for twenty-five years and not only taught but also coached the children of many residents of the district. The succession problem of following a very successful teacher would place a significant amount of pressure on the new teacher to be equally successful. The easiest succession occurs when a new teacher is replacing an unsuccessful teacher.

Compensation, Fringe Benefits, and
Rewards Associated With the Position

Regardless of what people say, the most qualified applicants will expect financial compensation that is comparable with positions in other school districts. The human resources department of a school district may also need to negotiate compensation and fringe benefits with desirable candidates. If the policies of a school district allow for flexibility in determining compensation and benefits, that district has a better possibility of attracting the most qualified members of Generation Y—particularly for hard-to-fill subjects such as mathematics and science. Districts that have a fixed-salary schedule and universal fringe benefits for all employees will have a more difficult time hiring Generation Y applicants.

Generation Y applicants are particularly attracted to positions that offer the opportunity to be rewarded for exceptional performance above and beyond the categorical types of compensation that are found in many or most school districts. Money, benefits, and working conditions motivate employees to greater levels of performance.

METHODS OF RECRUITING GENERATION Y

Not all recruitment methods produce the best candidates for a particular job vacancy or type of candidate. For this reason, before initiating the marketing and recruitment process, each job vacancy should be analyzed to discover what method will be most effective, particularly for recruiting Generation Y (Young, 2008). For example, an advertisement for Generation Y applicants should definitely appear on the school district's Web site. An advertisement in a local newspaper may not produce many candidates. Further, a school district recruiter who visits students at a four-year teacher education college in search of Generation Y candidates for a high school principal's position that requires a minimum of a master's degree in educational administration would be a waste of time.

Cybertechnology

It cannot be emphasized enough to both job seekers and human resources administrators in school districts that empirical evidence has demonstrated online recruiting produces results. Cybertechnology has transformed the recruiting process (Swann, 2006). School districts should be designing home pages that provide potential Generation Y employees with access to information about the school district, such as salary and fringe benefits, student-teacher ratios, and financial solvency. Student performance in terms of test scores and other information that can profile the student body is always a plus with Generation Y teachers. A potential

Generation Y employee should also have access to information about the application process and even the opportunity to fill out an application online. In addition, some applicants are maintaining their own Web sites full of teaching materials such as a teaching philosophy, sample lesson plans, and a résumé. In fact, many school districts use a Web-based application format through a state or county run agency, or through Web sites like www.edjoin.org or www.reap.org.

It can be expected that school districts with substandard salaries and fringe benefits probably will not provide such information on their Web sites, which, in turn, will discourage Generation Y job seekers from considering school districts that neglect to include such information.

When a school district has an unexpected vacancy, recruiting on the Internet should provide a good number of applicants in the shortest period of time. In addition, there are recruitment companies that post vacancies on the Internet, which allows Generation Y job seekers to submit a copy of their résumés on the site. This allows school district recruiters the ability to search the résumé bank on a daily or weekly basis in order to find suitable Generation Y candidates. Certainly, the greatest advantage to recruiting through the Internet is the ability to reach as many potential applicants as possible in the most cost-effective manner.

There is a rapidly growing approach to networking known as blogging, a form of online social interaction, that can be employed by Generation Y applicants to find the best school district to pursue when searching for a job. Also, there are networking services. Job seekers register with networking companies by supplying their names, locations, and employment status. Networking companies provide privacy and usually pledge not to sell personal information to a third party. This way, Generation Y potential employees add their names to an enormous list that can be accessed by employers and other applicants in the network. The objective is to find other people who live and work in places and organizations that interest a Generation Y job seeker. Even though there are different opinions about the effectiveness of online recruitment, no one can dispute the large number of people who are involved in Internet social networking.

Promoting From Within

Some school districts find it advantageous to train their own Generation Y employees for certain positions, which creates high morale among Generation Y employees. Promoting from within allows superintendents to have firsthand information about the in-house applicants. Generation Y teacher aides and substitute teachers can be promoted into full-time teaching positions when vacancies occur. Similarly, most large school districts have some classroom Generation Y teachers who are qualified to become principals.

There are disadvantages to following a system of promoting from within. Mediocre teacher aides and substitutes may be promoted into teaching positions while excellent individuals in the community are not considered. Also, affirmative action and equal employment opportunity requirements may dictate searching for personnel outside the organization. There is also the danger of inbreeding, which would hinder the infusion of new ideas and methods from Generation Y teachers who are new to the district.

Many school districts post job vacancies on Web site bulletin boards, in newsletters, or in special publications issued from the human resources or superintendent's office. This allows current Generation Y employees to apply for positions or to notify friends, relatives, and associates about vacancies.

Some large urban and suburban school districts are using a unique approach when they experience difficulty recruiting Generation Y teachers, particularly in science and mathematics. These districts are offering to pay a portion of the costs to acquire a college degree in order to hire staff members to fill Generation Y teacher vacancies. Generation Y teacher assistants have been targeted as a group of staff members who are likely to take advantage of this kind of program.

Referrals From Generation Y Teachers and Administrators

Perhaps the best source of identifying Generation Y candidates for teaching and administrator positions when a vacancy occurs comes from current Generation Y employees. There are a number of reasons for this observation. The most significant reason is that Generation Y employees will not usually recommend someone unless they believe that the referred person will do a good job, since their reputations as recommenders are at stake.

A good indicator of the quality of referrals from current Generation Y employees is the job performance of the recommender and his or her satisfaction with the school district as a whole. A recommendation from a Generation Y employee with inferior performance or from a Generation Y employee who is constantly complaining about the policies and procedures of the district should be carefully reviewed. Also, a Generation Y employee recommending a friend may also confuse friendship with potential job success. It is not uncommon for people to want friends in the workplace, both for social and economic reasons.

Beyond sociability, referrals from Generation Y teachers and principals often reflect professional rather than social contact. Membership in professional organizations such as the National Association of Secondary School Principals, the National Education Association, or the American Federation of Teachers gives people opportunities to become acquainted with the competencies of colleagues. Consequently, such referrals may be more credible than referrals based only on social contact.

A school district should establish a policy and procedure guideline that encourages Generation Y employees to recommend people for job vacancies. A common practice is for the Generation Y employees to provide their principal, superintendent, or the human resources department with the name(s) of potential candidates. The appropriate administrators can then send letters to the referred individuals, stating that they have been recommended to become candidates and inviting them to submit an application for the job. It should be noted that if the invitation is extended to become a candidate, an administrator must be very careful not to give the referred person the impression that the job is being offered.

Head-Hunting

In the business community, the practice of overtly recruiting individuals from other businesses is common. This is a practice that is often neglected in education because many educators see this as an inappropriate practice. However, this is not inappropriate if the searching district is not imposing undue pressure on the potential candidate.

Employment agencies fall into two categories, public or state agencies and private agencies. For all practical purposes, Generation Y teachers and administrators have made limited use of employment agencies in their searching for professional positions.

In 1933, a public employment service was established as a federal–state partnership. It was created not only to help individuals find suitable employment, but also to help employers find qualified workers. All fifty states have a state employment service agency with branch offices strategically located throughout each state. The U.S. Training and Employment Service supervises these agencies. The agencies provide services to those receiving unemployment benefits; benefits are available only to people who are registered with the state employment agency. Although state employment agencies are happy to list individuals with extensive training and highly developed skills, most people with such qualifications go to private agencies. Nevertheless, it is foolish for a school district not to list all vacancies with the appropriate state employment service agency because of the possibility that the right Generation Y employee may be registered. The financial outlay for such a listing is negligible, requiring nothing more than the cost of postage.

Private employment agencies, of course, charge a fee for their services. This fee may be charged to the employer, the Generation Y employee, or shared by both. The fee arrangement is usually dictated by the supply-and-demand principle. When applicants are abundant, potential Generation Y employees are usually required to absorb the fee. When applicants are scarce, the employers pay the fee.

Another major difference between public and private employment agencies is in the scope of services provided. Private agencies not only advertise and screen applicants for a job, but also provide a guarantee against unsatisfactory performance for a specified period of time, usually six to twelve months. If a particular Generation Y employee does not work out, the agency will place the employee elsewhere and find the company another employee without a fee.

Institutions of Higher Education

Most colleges and universities offer placement services not only to recent graduates, but also to former graduates. The most important service available in these placement departments is the maintaining of a personal file containing references, transcripts, and other pertinent documents. Thus, each time employees leave a position they may request the supervisor and other colleagues to send letters of reference to the placement service. This, in turn, will alleviate the burden of requesting former employers and colleagues to write reference letters each time an application is made for a different job. The placement service simply duplicates the references and sends them to prospective employers at the request of the graduate.

In terms of recruiting, listing vacancies with college and university placement services will easily reach recent Generation Y graduates. Further, because Generation Y teachers and administrators seeking jobs in school districts seldom use private or public employment agencies, college and university placement services are the best sources for finding potential Generation Y candidates for professional positions.

Most college and university placement services also sponsor job fairs at which school district administrators can meet potential Generation Y teachers. It is an opportunity for recruiters to highlight the positive aspects of their school districts in order to attract quality applicants. Some school districts that are having a difficult time recruiting Generation Y teachers may be given the authority by their respective boards of education to make a job offer to qualified candidates at these events.

Professional Organizations

Many professional organizations provide limited placement services for their members, including Generation Y members. These organizations either publish a roster of job vacancies or notify individual members concerning potential jobs. They usually list job vacancies in the classified section of their publications. However, having a classified section advertising jobs in a professional publication is common only to those organizations representing a specialty in educational administration. Professional education administration organizations include the American Association of School Personnel Administrators (AASPA), Association for Supervision and Curriculum Development (ASCD), Association of School Business Officials (ASBO), Council of Educational Facility Planners International (CEFPI), National Association of Elementary School Principals (NAESP), National Association of Pupil Personnel Administrators (NAPPA), National Association of Secondary School Principals (NASSP), National School Boards Association (NSBA), and National School Public Relations Association (NSPRA).

Walk-In Applicants

Unsolicited or walk-in applicants provide another avenue for obtaining potential Generation Y applicants. Although affirmative action requirements usually dictate advertising most positions, walk-in applicants can be good candidates—in particular because often they have been recently relocated to the area. Most unsolicited applicants contact the school district either by e-mail, by telephone, or in person. It is important to inform such individuals of the potential for employment with the district and to present them with applications to be filled out. If a vacancy occurs that fits an applicant's qualifications, that individual should then be contacted and invited to activate the application by written notification.

Minority, Women, and Other Protected Groups

Every school district has a Generation Y minority population, such as underutilized Generation Y females and qualified Generation Y people with disabilities. These populations can be serviced by media resources to recruit candidates from these groups. For example, in the southwestern United States, there are many local radio stations that are directed to the Mexican American population. Advertising vacancies on these radio stations can be a valuable method of recruiting Generation Y candidates.

Marketing the Position in Print

When a school district has a vacancy, it usually develops a formal advertisement. This advertisement can be used to implement the various methods of marketing and recruitment. It can easily be targeted to specific types of candidates, like Generation Y job seekers. The content of an advertisement is determined by the job description and criteria that will be used in selecting the most qualified candidate for the position. An advertisement must accurately reflect the major responsibilities of the position and the minimum qualifications, while still being brief enough to appear in newspapers, newsletters, or professional publications. This process ensures that affirmative action and equal employment opportunity requirements are properly fulfilled.

SUMMARY

After the administrative staff identifies current and future human resources needs, the next step is to market and recruit qualified personnel. There are constraints on marketing and recruitment that must be taken into consideration: diversity and affirmation action requirements, the reputation of the school district, and the salary and fringe benefits opportunities.

Generation Y applicants, of course, have different interests, abilities, and personalities than previous generations. For Generation Y, life and work satisfaction depends on how well individuals can utilize their abilities and find outlets for their interests, personality traits, and values.

The most common methods of recruiting Generation Y teachers and administrators are internal searches, referrals, contacting employment agencies, advertising vacancies with college and university placement services or job fairs, advertising on the Internet, advertising in newspapers and in the publications of professional organizations, following-up with unsolicited applications, and contacting community organizations that promote the interests of minority groups.

CASE STUDY

Mr. Mitchell is the director of human resources in a medium-sized suburban school district. The district is very financially stable because the taxpayers have been very responsive to the needs of the school district. They are first-generation college graduates with high academic expectations for their children.

However, the school district is beginning to change in the sense that the value of homes in the school district have significantly appreciated within the past ten years. Thus, the price of homes is generally outside the financial reach of younger families. Consequently, the district is experiencing a decline in students because the current residents are staying in their homes even though their children have graduated and have moved on to colleges and universities. Their homes are paid for and they are comfortable staying where they are.

A second phenomenon has also occurred. The current teachers, staff members, and administrators are middle-aged and older. There are a significant number of employees who will be retiring within the not-too-distant future. Because the school district has solid financial resources and good support from residents and particularly parents, the compensation, fringe benefits, and working conditions have been excellent. As such, the turnover of teachers, staff members, and administrators has been minimal.

Student achievement has been outstanding in relation to state criterion and close to 85 percent of the students go on to colleges and universities.

The expectation of the parents is reflected in the behavior and values of not only the students, but also all employees of the school district.

Mr. Mitchell and his human resources staff, however, are in the process of developing the job descriptions, school district Web site advertisement, and newspaper advertisement to replace six teachers, two administrators, and eight staff members. Twelve of the employees are retiring and four are leaving the district for other positions. The superintendent of schools and the members of the board are concerned about the fact that such a large number of new employees will need to be hired and also that this will be the beginning of other significant turnover in the immediate future. They know that such turnover could have a significant influence on the culture of the school district. The superintendent and the board are acutely aware of the media hype surrounding the cultural differences of Generation Y.

To address this concern, the superintendent has convened a committee composed of parents, teachers, staff members, and administrators to investigate and consider the method for marketing and recruiting Generation Y employees, and the criteria that should be used to select the replacements. As the director of human resources, the superintendent has selected Mr. Mitchell to be the chairperson of the committee.

Analyze the scenario described above by answering the following questions:

- What resources should Mr. Mitchell make available to the committee members in order to get them started?
- What are the ways he should organize the tasks of the committee?
- What do you think should be the expected outcomes of the committee's deliberations?
- If any, what are concerns may be important for Mr. Mitchell to address?

EXERCISE

1. As director of human resources amidst a district shortage of qualified Generation Y applicants for all types of positions in a district of 2,000 students, you have scheduled a meeting with the administrative staff, teacher representative, and support staff representative in order to elicit their assistance in recruiting applicants. Outline, in writing, your presentation and develop five discussion questions that will help you interact with them about this issue.

2. Obtain a copy of the advertisements for administrative, teaching, and support services positions in local school district Web sites and newspapers. Analyze them in relation to the information presented in this chapter.

3. In person or on the telephone, interview a human resources administrator from a school district who seems to be successful in marketing and recruiting Generation Y teachers and other employees to ascertain his or her opinion about the reasons why the district is successful.

CHAPTER FOCUS QUESTIONS

1. Given the fact that many of the teachers, staff members, and administrators that will be hired in the immediate future will be members of Generation Y, what marketing and recruitment strategies do you think are the most effective in recruiting Generation Y applicants?

2. What are the cybertechnological techniques that are likely to be used by Generation Y applicants?

3. What factors influence members of Generation Y to become applicants in certain school districts?

4. What are the elements that make up an effective marketing and recruitment Web site and/or other advertisements?

5. What is the advantage of using marketing and recruitment brochures or Web sites for certain positions?

3

Culture of the School as Generations Merge

Chapter Objectives

- To understand the importance of school culture
- To explore how veteran and new teachers work together
- To understand the characteristics of a positive school culture
- To gain knowledge in how to build a learning community

Vignette

Dr. Alverez is the principal of a junior high school that is about to switch into a middle school—redefining its mission and goals to suit the changing needs of students, parents, and the surrounding community. As part of this transition, Dr. Alverez realizes that using the middle school concept, many teachers will be placed in teams, and that school culture will be even more important than before. He is concerned about all of his teachers and how they will work together during this transition—in particular, because he knows of some "cliques" and "situations" that have occurred before in the school.

To make the transition and expectations as clear and pertinent as possible, Dr. Alverez decides to create a planning tool that he can use over the next few years to create a strong school culture. This planning tool can help any principal in analyzing current and incoming staff. For example, he uses a matrix identifying current staff, number of years experience at the school, number of years experience total, types of experiences utilizing

> the middle school concept, types of teamwork experiences, existing alliances, existing professional collaborations, existing rivalries, etc. Dr. Alverez decides that a planning tool like this will help him place teachers in workable teams while fostering the culture of the school. He can later add to it as needed with new hires. He also realizes that he may need to add content to the matrix as needed. For example, he may decide that it's important to list characteristics of each teacher such as their comfort level with technology, comfort level with team teaching, comfort level interacting with parents, etc. as he works on creating teams that support and benefit from working together. An example of a matrix like this appears below:

Teacher	Number of years experience total	Number of years experience at the school	Types of experiences utilizing the middle school concept	Types of teamwork experiences	Existing alliances	Existing professional collaborations
Mrs. Kramer						
Mr. Mitchell						
Mr. Bridgway						

CHARACTERISTICS OF GENERATION Y

Understanding Generation Y characteristics will help principals, superintendents, and other members of the school district community to understand the manner in which Generation Y teachers and administrators impact the culture of a school district and how the district's culture impacts Generation Y (Coomes & Debard, 2004; Half, 2008).

Generation Y is certainly adventuresome, but in a manner that is somewhat different than other generations. They definitely enjoy collaboration to the degree that it involves continual involvement with other teachers and administrators. They want to know what other professionals know and think about the issues that arise during the performance of their responsibilities. In a sense, they prefer to have a work area rather than an office because an office is somewhat isolating (Coomes & Debard, 2004; Half, 2008).

Generation Y teachers and principals certainly have all the inclinations toward religion and spirituality that other generations have had, but their inclination is slightly different. From their point of view, religion is practiced more in terms of religiosity. Members of Generation Y are observant of the tenets of specific religious doctrine, morality, and ritual but still understand that the foundation of their religiosity rests on a spirituality that goes beyond certain religions. Their spirituality searches for meaning and purpose when the recitation of doctrinal formulas or rituals is less than fulfilling. Their ontological instincts and experience with others inform their religious beliefs. Thus, religion is laced with a hope in the goodness of humans and the meaningfulness of just ordinary living. The disposition of a person toward human development is certainly a prerequisite for teachers and principals in their daily contact with children and colleagues (Coomes & Debard, 2004; Half, 2008).

Generation Y teachers and administrators also tend to look at the phenomenon of change in a different way. Rather than dealing with the consequences of change, they seek ways to precipitate change and often embrace change as something not only to be expected but also as exciting, as long as they see the value and worth in the change. Thus, new models for developing curricula and new curricular materials are often welcomed and present desired challenges to Generation Y teachers and principals. More fundamental to embracing change, Generation Y see themselves as being altered by the change and even enriched. To a certain degree, they conceptualize themselves as being reinvented, rather than bothered, by change (Coomes & Debard, 2004; Half, 2008).

The same perspective concerning the notion of "becoming" seems to be present in the worldview of Generation Y teachers and administrators. They tend to have an evolutionary worldview that compels them to see the world as being a dynamic environment, which is constantly changing and progressing. They make decisions based on the historical moment, which means that some conclusions may change because of increased knowledge and experience. They are inductive thinkers. While many of these characteristics are present in the worldviews of prior generations, some teachers and administrators see the human phenomenon as a finished product. Thus, they have a high degree of certitude about what they need to do in their professional lives because conclusions are always the same. They are deductive thinkers (Coomes & Debard, 2004; Half, 2008).

METHODS FOR ANALYZING SCHOOL AND DISTRICT CULTURE

One of the major reasons that teachers leave the profession early is the lack of collegial support and a strong sense of teamwork in the school (Futernick, 2007, p. 2). There needs to be a mutually supportive approach to teaching and instruction between all teachers and administrators to encourage positive culture. In fact, the teachers who remain in schools for their careers often cite the importance of community and distributed leadership, including joint decision making for the progress of the school.

In fact, despite which generation teachers come from, some of the characteristics they describe as contributing to job satisfaction are directly linked to the principal. For example, teachers appreciate principals who get involved in teaching, are sounding boards for teachers, provide positive feedback and support, and promote and support professional development. Knowing this, how can administrators assess or analyze their school cultures?

First and foremost, the administrator should talk to teachers and support staff about what they like about the school and what they dislike. While there will always be "extreme" cases or answers to this question, the administrator will obtain an overall "feel" for how teachers perceive the culture. This is particularly important as Generation Y teachers become part of the school as teachers or administrators. One common technique is to survey the teachers, conduct focus groups, or have a discussion at a faculty meeting (depending on the size of the faculty). Another way to build positive morale is to ask teachers to list two–three things they really like about the school and working there, and one–two things they would like to see changed. This focuses on the positive while also letting administrators see where people feel improvements or changes can be made. After doing this, administrators can also do the same with students or parents to get a feel for how satisfied or dissatisfied they are with the school. Another technique for analyzing school culture is to ask students and teachers what one word they think of when they think about the school or the school's culture. If teachers mainly state things like, "depressing," "overworked," or "a sad state," then administrators know they must start working toward a positive culture. If teachers and/or students are generally happy by analysis of their one-word answers, then administrators can focus their efforts on finding out what things would make a good school even better!

Another helpful way to assess school culture is to look at the mission of the school or district and see if the school and its teachers are working toward that mission or a school improvement plan. Continual assessment of a school and its offerings are important; this data can help an administrator understand the culture of the school. A common thought is that a principal only hears from parents, students, and teachers who are very upset or overall happy. Often, "the complainers" can overtake a principal's scheduled times and appointments. Therefore, it is important that the administrator for a school or district assess *overall* what teachers, parents, and students feel about the school and try not to be swayed by the negativity that may come with some conversations.

One phenomenological approach to analyzing culture uses the following four dimensions: describing, listening, reading, and observing (Rebore, 2003, pp. 148–156). These dimensions are not analyzed separately in order; instead, they are utilized simultaneously to understand school culture. Therefore, an administrator will examine school culture by describing events, listening to others, reading pertinent materials, and observing particular behaviors. For example, a new principal wants to analyze the school culture as it relates to extracurricular activities. Thus, she begins by attending some of the more popular extracurricular activities herself, such as observing football and soccer practices, attending choir practices, and watching the debate club. She describes the routines that she sees in each of these activities. She describes how individuals react to each other, if teamwork is present, if students and coaches or teachers are respectful of each other, and if an overall positive feeling emerges. Next, she listens to conversations between team members, students, and coaches or teachers to see if positive reactions take place. She also reads documents such as handbooks for coaches or handbooks for debate protocol. She also sees how many students are present in the various activities. Lastly, from all of these sources and her own observations, she synthesizes what type of culture emerges for the extracurricular activity programs.

"NEW AND OLD" COMING TOGETHER

As stated above, it is crucial that teachers work well together in a building. Issues that often affect good relations among teachers include lack of administrative leadership, instructional practices, unethical conduct, formation of cliques, and responsibility divisions (Gallagher, Bagin, & Morre, 2005, pp. 93–95). Lack of leadership allows for major differences among teachers to surface, often leading to rivalry, formation of cliques, major disagreement, and lack of respect among various teachers. Instruction practices that differ in the extreme can be problematic as overall instructional practices often lead to school culture. While some instructional differences will always exist among teachers, a lack of respect for those differing practices can lead to a divide among the teachers. This is particularly important as Generation Y enters schools with their technological superiority to many veteran teachers. Administrators must lead this meshing together of technology in teaching so that Generation Y teachers can use their skills effectively and show veteran teachers some of the new technologies; at the same time, veteran teachers should be expected to help mentor and show young teachers other issues and teaching skills they have used for years. Malicious gossip and rumors are considered unethical behavior—teachers must remember that they are professionals and treat each other with respect. Creating a professional working environment assists in the avoidance of cliques. Team teaching or grade teams can work effectively as long as social cliques do not occur alongside. Of course, certain teachers will be good friends, and groups of friends often eat together, etc. This only becomes a problem when people single out individuals and do not treat them appropriately, such as not making room for one more person at the lunch table or ending conversations as another teacher approaches. If teachers expect their students to work in harmony, they must demonstrate by example. Lastly, division of responsibility is crucial to avoid the previously mentioned issues that negatively affect teacher relations. An administrator must carefully divide teaching loads, types of classes and classrooms, and other responsibilities so as to prevent resentment among teachers who deem their loads unfair.

Because there are different characteristics among various generations in how they interact with each other, it is important for an administrator to be aware of these. In order for an administrator to understand these differences, descriptions of the two previous generations are required. For the most part, workers today come from three primary generations: The Baby Boomers, Generation X, and Generation Y. The "Traditionalists," or "Silent Generation," is the generation preceding the Baby Boomers. While many of them are still alive, most are retired. Therefore, it is important that we discuss the differences between Baby Boomers, Generation X, and Generation Y since these are the groups from which teachers will be mixed.

Baby Boomers (those born roughly between 1946 and 1965) currently make up the largest percent of the working population (although this is beginning to switch as the earlier Baby Boomers enter retirement). This generation is marked as one who fought for civil rights and world peace. They are very vocal, and they have been the wealthiest generation to date with the growth of the stock market and strong economy throughout their lives (Wong & Wong, n.d.). Generation X (roughly the generation between Baby Boomers and Generation Y) have characteristics that are a mix between Baby Boomers and Generation Y. Generation X entered the workforce with somewhat of a lazy stereotype. However, they soon found they had to work hard for themselves with a poorer economy, and higher poverty and divorce rates. Many from this generation used technology to their advantage creating Netscape, Amazon, etc., but did not rely on it for daily communication and interaction.

Generation Y, as was discussed at length in Chapter 1, is considered a generation of global and technically savvy citizens. They are generally socially conscious and feel they can make a difference in the world, alongside detailed and constructive plans for the future, as they feel others should value their worth and appreciate their talents. They have regularly been praised by parents. They generally work well in teams, and like constant feedback. They like to plan for the future and take a genuine interest in the organization for which they work. Furthermore, they have been challenged since birth to become critical thinkers and problem solvers. However, employers report that they typically require much oversight, avoid creative risks, and are too attached to their parents (Howe & Strauss, 2007, p. 52).

DeBard (2004) provides good examples of views toward issues by all three generations. For example, regarding trusting others, Baby Boomers are confident in themselves and do not necessarily trust authority. Generation X have low trust toward authority, and Generation Y have higher trust toward authority. Regarding evaluation, Baby Boomers expect formal evaluation at least once a year with documentation. Generation X typically expect the worst and ask how they are doing at review time, and

Generation Y expect feedback when they want it. Regarding education, Baby Boomers wanted freedom of expression, Generation X felt education was practical, and Generation Y young adults see education as a structure of accountability (p. 40).

The Office of Diversity at Honolulu Community College (n.d.), as part of their Web site on faculty development, offers some tips for working with Baby Boomers, including: pay attention to body language in communication; speak clearly and directly without being overpowering; be prepared to answer follow-up questions when discussing issues; and be flexible in thinking. Some tips for working with Generation Y include: use e-mail and short sound bites for constant communication; expect feedback and give feedback regularly; speak to them as equals. Some characteristics of Generation X are that they prefer a more informal style than Baby Boomers and use e-mail regularly, and they tend to work and problem solve without as much feedback as Generation Y. Given the various strategies that correspond to the differing characteristics, how does it work when you put all these people together in a school?

An administrator must be aware of differences and understand various generations. An administrator may be wise to have a conversation with veteran and new teachers about different generation expectations so that there are clearer understandings. Likewise, an administrator cannot expect the same things from all people. While all teachers may use e-mail as an expectation, administrators should know that they may get quicker feedback from Baby Boomers by walking down to their classrooms and talking, while they may get quicker feedback from Generation Y teachers by e-mailing.

Another aspect administrators must be aware of is the difference in teaching and learning expectations between the generations. This is crucial in light of the fact that the majority of new teachers in a school will be Generation Y teachers. Most Generation Y teachers entering the profession today arrive with strong critical-thinking skills. Because of this, they should be mentored slightly differently than Baby Boomers or Generation X would have been mentored in the past. These new teachers benefit more from team mentoring or study groups than one-on-one mentoring (Wong & Wong, n.d.). Generation Y teachers like to collaborate in developing ideas related to curriculum and academics. In teaching, which is often a lonely profession, Generation Y teachers must be provided opportunities to discuss and collaborate with others during their first years of teaching or be allowed to teach using the team framework. Having been brought up using cooperative learning and other teamwork strategies, they must not be expected to teach alone all day, every day, without time for interaction with mentors or a mentoring team. While Generation Y teachers are achievement oriented, they also need structure. With boundaries, they expect constant feedback and praise when appropriate. They appreciate the experience of veteran teachers, but they also want their ideas heard and taken seriously.

Some other issues include formality of dress and titles used. The formality of dress has changed over time—beginning at one time with all female teachers wearing skirts and all male teachers wearing ties. Some schools now have a teacher "uniform" that may include a school polo shirt and khaki pants. Formality of dress is typically culturally driven and can vary from school to school. It is imperative that all teachers, including newly hired Generation Y teachers, understand the school dress culture and respond accordingly. Another issue of similar concern is how teachers are addressed in the school. Some schools always use Mr., Mrs., or Miss followed by last name—even when teachers address each other informally. Other schools use first names with titles; sometimes cultures exist where students address teachers differently than teachers address other teachers. As is the case with dress, newly hired teachers should respond accordingly by using titles as deemed appropriate in the school culture.

While the culture of any school exists, it is always slightly changing as teachers and students come and go. It is crucial that administrators move their schools in a positive direction as these changes occur. For example, with the major increase in technology in teaching, it is crucial that the administrator encourage and support all teachers to use technology appropriately—and not for technology's sake. Administrators should also encourage all generations to work together and point out to veteran teachers that they may be required to provide constant feedback as mentors for new teachers, but also spend some time learning new technologies from these new teachers. Likewise, Generation X or Y teachers may need to show others technologies they use, but also realize that Baby Boomers have much experience from which they can learn. Respecting and communicating effectively between generations leads to a positive school climate.

CHARACTERISTICS OF A POSITIVE SCHOOL CULTURE

School leaders cannot be strong instructional leaders without hiring and retaining good teachers. School administrators must create a positive school environment where strong relationships exist among staff. Aside from superintendents, the most crucial administrators to build a supportive culture are the building principals (Gallagher et al., 2005, p. 92). Their attitudes and actions often determine the way others perceive the school system and school culture. In what ways is a school culture seen as positive? First and foremost, the principal must have good communication skills and personal human interaction skills. In other words, principals must be able to listen, talk, direct, and offer advice as appropriate. Rather than a domineering figure, the principal must be seen as a leader working together with effective teachers. Principals must show true compassion toward their staff; in return, the staff should see the principal as someone whom they can trust and confide. Not only must principals say they are good at human interactions, they must show it in daily actions. This "spirit of goodwill" will resonate within the school and generate a mutual respect, all contributing toward a positive school culture.

A positive school culture is one in which, overall, the teachers are satisfied with their working conditions. One problem for some administrators is the concept that satisfaction and dissatisfaction are connected to the same issues (Gallagher et al., 2005, p. 93). This is not the case. Herzberg (1959, as cited by The Internet Center for Management and Business Administration, 2007) researched job satisfaction and developed key understandings of the differences between satisfaction and dissatisfaction among workers; his theory is called the motivation-hygienic theory. The components of satisfaction (motivational needs) include achievement, recognition, work itself, responsibility, advancement, and growth. Components of dissatisfaction (hygienic needs) include policy, administration, salary, work conditions, and interpersonal relations with administrators and fellow colleagues. Most important, however, is the concept that being satisfied is not the opposite of being dissatisfied, and vice versa. The opposite of satisfaction is no satisfaction; similarly, the opposite of dissatisfaction is no dissatisfaction. Therefore, in order for teachers to move from dissatisfaction in their jobs to satisfaction, both lists of needs must be addressed. This is crucial knowledge for the administrator who must provide a culture where both needs are met. If a culture exists where the hygienic needs are met, teachers may be working satisfactorily but will not be working to their full potential.

Another issue mentioned previously that can seriously affect school culture is the relations among teachers in a building or district. Teachers must be supportive of each other, even if they have different teaching styles, opinions, or are of varying ages. It is crucial that teachers of all generations work together to not only provide a positive learning environment for the students, but also a positive working environment—both which contribute to the overall culture of the school.

BUILDING LEARNING COMMUNITIES

The key component to building learning communities is to understand that leadership is a shared responsibility among administrators, parents, teachers, staff members, students, community leaders, and citizens of the surrounding community (Rebore & Walmsley, 2007, pp. 81–92). Every school is a reflection of the community it serves. Thus, every school culture is a reflection of the members of that community. While many educators and citizens think of the school as a separate entity, in reality, schools and communities interact regularly. This provides an opportunity to build an effective learning community. In order to lead a professional learning community, the following attributes of culture must be analyzed: leadership, collaboration, focus on learning, goal development, school improvement, celebration, and persistence (Ubben, Hughes, & Norris, 2001, p. 29). First, however, a clear mission must be identified for the school. This mission should consist of a shared vision and goals between the school, teachers, stakeholders, parents, and the community. Therefore, the mission must be based not only on what the school feels is important, but also what the community and its culture feel is important. This mission should be the backbone of a school improvement plan and constantly focus on positive education for all students.

While stakeholders come together to frame a school's mission, politics can sometimes be a deterrent. Some community groups may want to promote their own individual purpose above others; therefore, it is crucial that a leader continues to formulate mission around common purposes for the good of the school and community. As Generation Y becomes part of the community and school, changes should be made accordingly. A learning community can set a basic framework, but it is a continual process. Who are the members of a learning community? First, they are the students, teachers, and parents of children in school. But, they can also be members of the community who use the school in some way. For example, citizens who support the school band or attend school football games are part of the learning community. Nurses or doctors who provide immunizations or tobacco-prevention programs to students are also part of the learning community. As with school culture, it is important that each member of the learning community develops trust and respect for other members. "It takes a village to raise a child" is synonymous with the idea of a learning community.

In order for a learning community to be effective, open communication must be present (communication is discussed in more detail in Chapter 4). The school administrator is often the person leading communication between members of the learning community. It is crucial that administrators use straightforward language with members of the learning community since noneducators may not understand education "lingo." Many of the techniques described above regarding positive school culture and communication relate here: an administrator must be genuine and respectful in communicating with everyone. Furthermore, collaboration is key to a successful learning community (Busher, 2005, 461–462). The most effective learning communities are those that utilize distributed leadership among their teachers.

Technology has made mass communication among the learning community easier. An interactive school Web site, discussion board, or newsletters are just a few examples of how the community can work together. In particular, Generation Y teachers expect these types of communications. One aspect of Generation Y teachers, discussed in Chapter 1, is the issue of constant feedback. These teachers expect responses from administrators or other teachers as they work. This could also affect their work with other learning community members. These teachers regularly keep in contact with parents, and may solicit parental help or community involvement in the classroom on a regular basis. This constant communication helps new and veteran teachers interact effectively using the principle of subsidiarity.

"Subsidiarity as a principle suggests that, wherever possible, decision making should take place at the point closest to the people not the other way around" (Mason & Randell, 1995, p. 24). This concept basically states that distributed decision making is necessary and should be executed at the most appropriate level. For example, if the administration must make a decision about traditional vs. block scheduling, the teachers would be the ones who know the systems and their students the best to determine if one version over another would be best in their school. While board members or the principal can make recommendations, it may be best to form a committee of those most affected (teachers, students, or counselors) to investigate the matter.

Most importantly, the most effective schools and learning communities are those led by administrators who are not dictatorial, but instead, people who listen and collaborate with others while facilitating the work of various members of the learning community. In order for administrators to be effective in schools, they must be competent and trusted. These are components that administrators prove by their actions in a learning community.

HIRING FOR MISSION

Newly hired teachers are interested in the leadership style of their new principal or superintendent in addition to the type of school and community, and part of effective hiring is hiring individuals whom fit the culture of the school and learning community. This is what should be described as "hiring for mission." All schools should have a mission statement that encompasses what is important to the members of that learning community. In addition, it is crucial that there is periodic review of the mission to prevent stagnation. Hiring Generation Y teachers for mission enhances the learning-community culture of schools and school districts. Every school has a different nuance of the learning community and "the fit" is important for teachers if they are going to become contributing members of the community.

This is *not* to say that principals should only hire teachers who are exactly like other teachers in the building. Rather, administrators must hire individuals who fundamentally believe in the mission of the school and work well with individuals in the school and the community. For example, assume that one school's mission centers completely on teaching using the theory of multiple intelligences. Therefore, the culture of the school is established with teachers using many forms of multiple intelligences in any single lesson. In addition, parents are accustomed to this type of teaching and expect it. If a teacher candidate is interviewed and has no understanding at all of multiple intelligences, or does not believe in the theory, then this applicant would not be a good fit for the school. Teachers who are hired and begin working in a school where they do not feel like "the fit" is good, ultimately leave to find more satisfaction in their careers. When administrators hire new teachers, they hope to hire ones who are happy in the positions, work well with other teachers, and teach toward the mission of the school. These teachers typically stay, resulting in less teacher turnover and the need for fewer temporary or short-term positions. This kind of stability enhances the school climate and decreases the demand of the administrator for hiring.

SUMMARY

Methods for analyzing school and school district culture are crucial as "new and old" teachers merge together each school year. Administrators must be able to communicate and work well with all generations of teachers to create a positive school climate. This is part of the larger learning community. Understanding learning communities and developing strategies for creating strong learning communities that include Generation Y adults and teachers will enhance a school culture. Lastly, hiring Generation Y teachers for mission is imperative to continue a positive school culture and learning community.

CASE STUDY A

Two schools (School 1 and School 2) are in neighboring districts in a state. The entire state has had limited funding for education. In particular, each district is experiencing funding problems for the upcoming school year. Therefore, the board of education in each district asked that administrators find a way to eliminate costs and reduce the budget. The teachers in each district are told that there is a major "budget crunch" for next year, and they are asked to submit ideas on how to lower the budget. Some teachers offer to not order as many supplies or reuse supplies from last year. Others offer to put off ordering new computers, calculators, and textbooks that had been in planning. Decreasing teacher-salary cost overall, administrators hire all newly graduated teachers for retiring teachers. Despite the budget cuts, morale in both schools is surprising high—mainly because of the culture to work together.

School 1: Teachers work together throughout the entire school year. Overall, the budget cut does not have a huge impact on the school culture.

School 2: The teachers start the year by working hard together. However, near the end of the school year, the district buys new furniture and puts air conditioning in the district offices.

Analyze the scenarios described above by answering the following questions:

- How do you think school culture changed in School 2?
- What differences in school culture do you think there were between School 1 and School 2 at the end of the year?
- How do you think the situations affected retention of teachers in both schools?
- What issues will the building administrators of School 2 have even though School 2's purchases were at the district level?
- How will the learning community be affected overall in both communities?

CASE STUDY B

Oak Grove Elementary School is a small elementary school in a rural Kansas town. It has four sections of each grade and Grades K–6 are in the building. Teachers in this area typically stay for most of their teaching career. Baby Boomers make up 55 percent of the teachers, Generation X make up 30 percent, and Generation Y (including next year's new hires) will make up 15 percent of the teachers. Most of the Baby Boomers have been at the school a long time, and most teach the upper-level grades. When others retire, the most senior teachers choose which grade level they would like to teach and are allowed to move if there is an opening. The principal traditionally has not moved teachers around unless they ask. What has happened over time is that the lower grades are taught by high-energy teachers who like to team teach and use technology; but, when the children get to higher grades, they are taught by very experienced and great teachers who do not use technology or the team approach as much. The principal decides that it would benefit the children and the school by mixing teachers up next year so that there is a mixture of generations teaching all grade levels.

At first, teachers are upset because many who like a particular grade may be asked to change. Thus, the principal, rather than simply forcing people to move grades and completely upsetting the staff, announces the changes and explains how the positions will be allocated. He asks teachers to rank the grades they would like to teach in order. He then asks each teacher to list one–two particular teachers he or she would like to teach with (and one of the two must be a teacher of a different age). This will force teachers to analyze, with some degree of choice, whom they might like to teach with and what they might like to teach. The principal also recognizes that not all preferences may be honored, and those teachers who do not get their preferences will have first say in movement the following year. The principal hopes that by rearranging in this way, teachers of differing generations may bring attributes to the grade-level team that enable all to work effectively together.

Analyze the scenarios described above by answering the following questions:

- In what ways will school culture be changed positively and negatively?
- What types of technology do you think the Generation X and Generation Y teachers can bring to all levels of the classroom?
- What benefits are there to placing Baby Boomer teachers at every grade level?
- What benefits are there to placing at least one teacher who is very proficient in technology at each grade level?
- How will moving all the teachers around and creating new interactions affect collaboration?
- How will Generation Y teachers cope with being the smallest percent in the building?
- How will Generation X teachers who have only worked with Baby Boomers change now that they will be considered the "veteran" teacher in a new group that includes Generation Y teachers?
- What kinds of discussions about generational differences must the principal have with the teachers before school starts again?
- What differences in classroom instruction and professional growth should the principal expect to see at each grade level?
- Is this generational rearrangement a necessary and worthwhile task?

EXERCISE

After reading each situation, identify the feelings being expressed and the phenomenological dimension(s) of cultural analysis that the administrator must use to analyze culture: describing, listening, reading, and observing. Also decide what would be the most appropriate response to continue promoting a positive culture.

Situation 1

The principal notices that a newly hired teacher in the science department is struggling with discipline in some of his classes. In passing, the principal asks the new teacher's mentor how everything is going with the mentoring process, and she says everything is fine.

Feelings: _____

_____

Cultural analysis dimension: _____

_____

Response: _____

_____

Situation 2

The second-grade team has the option of getting a SMART board for each second-grade classroom for next year. Three of the teachers are veteran teachers, and one of the teachers in this team is in his first year of teaching. The new teacher really would like a SMART board but the veteran teachers are reluctant to get them.

Feelings: _____

_____

Cultural analysis dimension: _____

_____

Response: _____

_____

Situation 3

Many of the students at Rockwell Elementary School have parents from Generation X. However, most of the teachers are from the Baby Boomer generation. The parents have asked repeatedly that the teachers e-mail updates about children and utilize a school e-newsletter. The teachers have resisted and prefer telephone or face-to-face conversations. The principal must find a happy medium.

Feelings: _____

_____

Cultural analysis dimension: _____

_____

Response: _____

_____

Situation 4

A new principal in a middle school realizes that the sixth-grade team is not "welcoming" their newest Generation Y teacher very well. Even though they include her in team meetings, they constantly whisper to one another. They are also good friends and meet regularly outside school. The principal sees the newest teacher wiping her eyes in her classroom one day after a team meeting and believes she may have been crying.

Feelings: _____

_____

Cultural analysis dimension: _____

_____

Response: _____

_____

Situation 5

Deciding that the English department at a high school needs new textbooks, the administrators of one large high school order all new English textbooks for Grades 9–12 over the summer. When teachers arrive at "back to school orientation," the principal proudly announces the new textbooks. However, the feedback from the teachers is not positive because they are not the books they would have chosen.

Feelings: _____

_____

Cultural analysis dimension: _____

_____

Response: _____

_____

Situation 6

The school district offers a new and fantastic early-retirement package, and one-third of the teachers in one building take the package and retire over the span of three years. The school then hires Generation Y teachers to replace the Baby Boomers who took the retirement package. The principal sees opportunity for cultural change, and wonders what may change in the school.

Feelings: _____

_____

Cultural analysis dimension: _____

_____

Response: _____

_____

CHAPTER FOCUS QUESTIONS

1. Describe the learning community in your school today, and then describe the learning community you hope to have in five years. What are the key differences?

2. Apply and describe the principle of subsidiarity to a situation in your school.

3. What are some measures you can take in your own school to begin to alter school culture to be more positive?

4. If you were able to create any school mission statement, what would it be?

5. Can you state your school mission without referencing it? What components are important for you in hiring teachers and how do these fit within the mission?

6. Provide a situation where you have seen a "bad fit" for a person in a school. What types of things were difficult for this person?

Communication Aspects of Generation Y Teachers

VIGNETTE

Pam Jankowski is a Generation Y graduate who begins her first teaching job in a school that has traditionally had teachers from the Baby Boomer generation. In fact, the principal describes the teaching staff as mainly "Boomers and Traditionalists." At the first faculty meeting in August, Pam opens her laptop and proceeds to take notes and use the Internet as appropriate during the meeting. Pam has always used technology in her education; in her college classes, she was encouraged to use it during class time to enhance her learning. For example, most students with laptops would participate in group discussions by being able to search the Web for clarification or examples of the topic for discussion for that class period. She also always took notes directly on handouts from the instructors posted to a university tool such as "Blackboard." Therefore, she was used to the complete integration of technology in her own professional learning and development.

At the meeting, when she pulled out her laptop and tried to find an outlet to connect, most of the teachers were shocked and did not understand why it was needed. After the meeting, some of the teachers approached the principal about the laptop and explained that they were "insulted" when others were using laptops during important meetings. They felt that one cannot pay total attention as needed with the distraction of the laptop. Thus, the principal banned laptops from all future staff meetings. Pam was appalled at what had happened. She wasn't sure how she could participate and stay engaged in the meetings with little support from the way she learned and the technology she was used to.

CHARACTERISTICS OF GENERATION Y

It should be evident that Generation Y teachers and principals are seriously and intensely involved in communicating by electronic means, which includes cell phones, iPods, text messages, e-mail, and Web sites. Further, such communication is carried out asynchronously, meaning that they are not tied to real time in their endeavor to communicate. The communication is instantaneous and dialogue can continue to whatever extent that the people desire through chat rooms. Of course, the danger in relying on electronic communication that is not tied to real time is the tendency to become isolated. That may seem difficult to understand since there is a flurry of communication taking place, but if we only communicate electronically and not in person, we may eventually know more information but not understand the person or persons with whom we are communicating (Half, 2008).

Electronic communication does not permit a holistic approach to communication that values verbal and nonverbal communications, which often reveals the true intention of the person with whom we are communicating, and the realms of emotions and feelings. Teachers and principals certainly need to communicate with children and colleagues in all areas: electronic writing, verbal, and nonverbal (Half, 2008).

However, in contrast to what was just stated, Generation Y teachers and administrators do have a desire for in-person communication. This is accomplished through collaboration and teamwork, which is highly valued. Specifically, Generation Y teachers and administrators want ongoing communication with their immediate supervisors, principals, or superintendents. Further, they want their principal or superintendent to be a person whom they respect and trust. Thus, transparency in management style is an important strategy in carrying out the responsibilities of being a principal or superintendent (Half, 2008).

MULTIPLE DIMENSIONS OF THE COMMUNICATION PROCESS

Communication occurs in multiple forms among multiple types of people. Communication has changed over the past fifteen years because of technology, and Generation Y understands this communication change well. Communication is also affected by the personalities of those involved. Therefore, responses to communication efforts are never the same by all people. The demeanor of the sender also can affect how communication is received. Communication among individuals occurs in four major forms: written, nonverbal, verbal, and cultural (Rebore, 2003, p. 129). The importance of culture and communication was described in Chapter 3. Written, nonverbal, and verbal communication will be described next.

Written communication is essential in any school or district. Because schools affect many people, and not all people can be present at all times, it is crucial that information is often spread to others through the written word. For example, if a new policy is adopted by the board of education, it is important that a written notice is sent to all teachers and parents. Since not all parents and teachers would have been present at the recent board meeting where the policy may have been approved, it is important that written information is provided in a timely manner to keep everyone abreast of changes and expectations. Furthermore, written communication may likely be the most important type of communication, because by its very nature, it is documented. Without recorded verbal communication, it is difficult to "prove" that one thing was said over another. However, by putting any communication in writing, "proof" is inevitable. This can benefit a teacher or administrator, but it can also be a detriment if the communication was not sent or accepted positively.

Verbal communication is equally important for human interaction. A school cannot have successful day-to-day operations without strong verbal communication. This includes communication from teachers to students and vice versa. It also includes teacher-to-teacher communication and teacher-to-administrator communication. On a daily basis, for a majority of the day, a teacher or administrator will speak on a number of issues. The problem with verbal communication is that it can be ambiguous. The receiver may not truly understand or interpret the way the sender indicated. Often people are misinterpreted, which can sometimes escalate into problems. Therefore, it is crucial that both administrators and teachers think about the perception of their comments, and adjust accordingly. Doing so will create a stronger and more positive culture.

Many would agree that nonverbal communication is equally as important as verbal communication. Nonverbal communication refers to the characteristics that individuals show while speaking (or not speaking) to others. For example, suppose that the principal is talking to the teachers about a new curriculum, and a teacher rolls her eyes. That nonverbal communication by the teacher negatively affects some because everyone can tell that she does not agree or has a problem with what the principal is saying. Likewise, if the principal hurriedly goes through the curriculum change when, in fact, it needs more time, then the nonverbal cues she is giving is that the curriculum may not be important. Obviously nonverbal communication can negatively affect a situation. However, it can also be positive such as clapping when a student does well on an exam.

Nonverbal communication can be divided into physical expressions, environmental expressions, and vocalizations (Rebore, 2003, p. 168). Physical expressions include facial expressions such as eye contact, posture, gestures, and movement. Some examples include placing hands on hips, slouching, rolling eyes, sitting upright, and smiling. Environmental expressions include the way people decorate their classrooms or personal materials. Vocalizations include crying, sighing, laughing, or changing tone of voice. Nonverbal communication is in almost every verbal exchange, and teachers and administrators often pay attention to not only what people say, but also how they say it, as this leads to more understanding about attitude.

Nonverbal communication is sometimes aligned with ethnicity or home culture. This makes it challenging for teachers and administrators who work with colleagues and students from many backgrounds and cultures. Most importantly, misunderstandings can occur. Therefore, it is crucial that administrators and teachers make sure that their ideas are communicated and understood clearly as best possible. For example, some people judge a person merely by the first handshake. It is important that administrators be clear and professional at all times: a strong handshake with direct eye contact will often begin a positive tone. The face of an individual provides more nonverbal communication than anything else, but sometimes it is difficult to know what the nonverbal communication means. Often, when others make direct eye contact they are trying to be very involved or engaged; avoiding eye contact can mean that a person is uncomfortable or feels uneasy. Having an open face with eye contact can begin a discussion in a positive manner. However, in some cultures, direct eye contact is often avoided; it is helpful for administrators to understand what may be the case for particular Generation Y teachers. Additionally, Generation Y has been criticized for not having good written, verbal, and nonverbal skills because of the influence of technology on their lives. It is important that a principal is aware of how this may change communication in the school. All teachers must find common ground for communication and respect and adapt accordingly.

Another nonverbal aspect by which others judge professionals is dress. An administrator or teacher who dresses professionally typically creates a more formal tone. Likewise, teachers who wear jeans regularly create a very informal tone. Depending on the culture of the school, dress should mimic the verbal communication of an individual.

When mixing written, verbal, and nonverbal communication, it is important to be professional at all times and choose the correct type of communication for the situation. For example, if administrators or teachers need time to respond to a situation, they would choose written communication. This allows time to rethink and formulate an appropriate response. Too often, individuals "fly off the handle" when verbally speaking about a controversial topic. Likewise, however, sometimes individuals write things in e-mail that they would not say face-to-face. It is important that at all times, teachers and administrators are professional and communicate appropriately. Remember, "although language is the principal tool in coding a message, still there are times when a body movement, a facial gesture, an unusual noise, or some other sign will convey just as much meaning to the receiver of the message" (Gallagher et al., 2005, p. 74).

NEW COMMUNICATION MEDIUMS

As schools changed tremendously over the past fifteen years because of technology, the communication media used by teachers toward both students and adults have also changed. In the 1980s, the major communication media in schools were face-to-face discussions, telephone conversations, and newsletters or handwritten notes sent home. With the increase in the availability of the personal computer in the1990s, newsletters and notes became word processing documents, and copying these with a professional copying machine created a more professional look than the old fashioned "ditto machine." Even though the concept of e-mail was developed prior to 1980, its use became widespread in the 1990s as computers became available to many. E-mail continued to become more popular as the World Wide Web developed in the early 1990s along with the use of portable laptops.

While many teachers used telephones to communicate with parents, often there were not individual phones in classrooms. Teachers had to use the phone in the main office or teachers' lounge with little privacy. Many schools currently have phones in classrooms, or allow the use of cellular phones by teachers. Cellular phones also became popular in the early 1990s as the cost lowered and availability of service drastically increased. This allowed more freedom for teachers to initiate phone calls as needed either in the classroom, on the playground, or in another part of the school building.

Some technological tools that teachers began to use in the 1990s, and still use, include the document camera, Webcams, digital files for television or computer, SMART board technology, and wireless headphones for students (a description of various technology terms can be found in the appendix). All of these were continually developed in the 1990s but have recently become more realistic purchases. With the large number of computers and wireless networks using broadband, teachers have access to an infinite number of resources from across the world. Instant messaging, skyping, or talking with others via the Internet also allows for conversations in real time between students or with others. The use of wikis, DVRs, blogs, WebQuests, podcasts, and webcasts have allowed teachers to select specific items to show students via a technological medium at any given time.

The opportunities available from all communication media have changed the ways teachers teach. Prior to 1990, "having knowledge" meant being educated and intelligent (Provenzo & Gotthoffer, 2000, p. 2). Today, everyone has access to the knowledge they need. This access is remarkably easy with the Internet. Thus, today's focus on education is not focused solely on knowing things, but also on problem solving and having the skills to search for knowledge while critically examining it. While most Generation Y teachers use this technology available to them immediately, some veteran teachers also have been using technology in different ways than before. An administrator must have knowledge of the various types of technology available, what teachers need and want, and how it benefits students. Regarding teaching, it is imperative that teachers use technology as an enhancement to teaching rather than a replacement to it.

Regardless of the teaching aspect of technology, communication between teachers and students, teachers and parents, and teachers and other education professionals is crucial. Strong communication skills are still necessary even with multiple options for technology. Communication continues to be what brings a connection between humans—making interactions very personal.

FREQUENCY AND CHARACTERISTICS OF COMMUNICATION

Communication methods and styles of Generation Y teachers are definitely different than those of past teachers. Baby Boomer teachers would have begun their teaching careers utilizing mainly verbal conversations and written documents. Generation X teachers began teaching with the expectation that some of this communication could take place via e-mail. Generation Y teachers now teach with the expectation that communication takes place in all forums: face-to-face, telephone, e-mail, texting, and through Web pages. Baby Boomers will often keep e-mails brief, preferring to talk with others to work through issues or to have conversations. Generation X teachers often keep a string of e-mails going until it gets too long (often thought of as more than three exchanges), and then meet the correspondent to talk face-to-face. Generation Y teachers often finalize many things via e-mail, preferring to have the time to respond as it suits their schedules. It is crucial that coteachers and administrators realize that Generation Y teachers grew up writing in the digital age. Thus, even though they were taught how to write with a pencil or pen and paper, the stress of good penmanship was never present; they do not often feel they need to write a handwritten note (Howe & Strauss, 2007, p. 187). In addition, while they know good spelling is an admirable characteristic, they are also happy to let the word processing program correct spelling for them. Therefore, a "happy medium" must exist between all.

Most would agree that face-to-face conversations are best when an issue is of utmost importance. Also, if the topic is controversial or people are arriving at the conversation upset or dissatisfied, face-to-face communication is often best. The simple reason why it is the best form of communication is that body language (nonverbal communication) can help with interpersonal relationships and communication. People are able to express themselves and clarify issues as needed. There is a tendency for some Generation X and Y individuals to "hide behind" e-mail. In other words, they send information through e-mail that they would not be confident explaining face-to-face. It is crucial that administrators know that their teachers understand when e-mail is appropriate and when it is not. Also, e-mail is a good forum for scheduling meetings, making announcements, getting initial ideas expressed, etc. However, teachers should never be "afraid" of approaching another teacher, parent, or administrator, and should not rely on e-mail as a substitute.

One major benefit of e-mail is that is gives the receiver of the e-mail time to formulate and respond. If an irate parent approaches a teacher or administrator face-to-face, a new teacher or administrator may feel flustered and not "think off the top of the head" well. If an irate parent sends an e-mail, the teacher or administrator has some time to think about the issue, create a plan of action to address the issue, and respond accordingly and professionally. However, a teacher or administrator must *always* be professional. If the response of the e-mail will make the situation worse, he or she should immediately request a meeting to work through issues. Another issue pertaining to professionalism is spelling and grammar. E-mail and texting have created a "shortened" and informal way of using the English language. Personal communication is often informal and quick— especially when texting. However, teachers and administrators must remember that professionally, they must use proper spelling and grammar when communicating via e-mail to parents or community members.

Generation Y teachers integrate technology in their lives so well because they have not really ever lived without it. Thus, it is natural to constantly communicate via e-mail, telephone, etc. without giving it a second thought. One issue, however, that needs a second thought is that of security. Teachers should only use secure networks when discussing students or private matters. Furthermore, e-mail is a form of written communication meaning that it can always be traced (even if someone thinks it's gone because it was "deleted" in the mail folder). Thus, a teacher or administrator must always be conscious of what is being written in the message since it ultimately is written documentation that could be used elsewhere (such as in a legal matter or in a newspaper if the message gets to the wrong person). With the familiarity of always using technology, Generation Y teachers must be cognizant of what information should be placed in an e-mail compared to what should not.

Another major benefit of e-mail as a communication forum is that teachers, administrators, and parents can communicate on their own time. Thus, if teachers or administrators do not have time to make telephone calls during the day, they may be able to e-mail in the evening—even past when "acceptable" telephoning times have passed. This allows more flexibility in communication. As a result, it often leads to more constant communication with quick feedback. Teachers and administrators are extremely busy during the school day; thus traditionally, it may have taken a teacher or administrator a few days to respond to a parent. With e-mail, parents and teachers are in constant communication about daily activities, absences, issues of concern for the child, etc. In many ways, e-mail has created a stronger home-school communication network.

One negative implication related to technology is the constant feeling of being "on-call." With landline phones, cellular phones, e-mail, and the Internet, teachers and administrators may never feel like they have any "downtime." Just as constant communication is important, it is equally important to set boundaries and guidelines for communication use. Teachers can explain to parents that they last check e-mail at 4 p.m., or will check once each evening, or that they do not check e-mail during the week-end. This creates clear guidelines about when parents can expect a response from a teacher. Expecting immediate responses at all times is an unrealistic expectation.

One complaint of many Generation Y young adults is their lack of good writing, spelling, and speaking skills. Because so much informal language is being used through technology, formal language skills may not be as strong as in the past. Generation Y teachers must keep this in mind as they work with older teachers, parents, administrators, and especially children. Again, teachers are professionals and are required to have good command of the English language in addition to being able to teach children strong communication skills. Poor English quickly creates a negative impression among fellow teachers, administrators, and parents.

MULTITASKING

Traditionally, widespread technology first referred to the radio followed by the television. Baby Boomers may remember their entire family sitting around the radio or television listening or watching a program together. Once the program was over, the radio or television would be turned off and another activity would resume. This concept is far from "normal" for Generation X or, in particular, Generation Y. Generation Y is used to doing a multitude of things at the same time. They may have the television on, while listening to their iPod, and doing some kind of work at the same time. Generation X started this trend of multitasking, but Generation Y has perfected it. Generation Y has been surrounded by neon flashing lights, sound bites, quick changes in television programming, and constant technology change. They are accustomed to watching one thing, listening to another, and yet doing a third or fourth thing. This can sometimes seem strange and nonproductive to older individuals.

Generation Y teachers may e-mail while planning a lesson, and are not as bothered when interrupted because they can quickly return to what they were doing. Administrators should be aware of this, in particular, as they interact regularly with many Generation Y teachers. Older administrators and teachers find communication among others distracting when they are presenting or discussing something. In contrast, Generation Y teachers expect to be able to communicate during a presentation, and even use their iPhone or laptop connected wirelessly to the Internet to look something up at the same time. It is crucial that administrators understand that Generation Y teachers are not necessarily being disrespectful, but are engaging in learning concurrently. Also important, Generation Y teachers should realize that if they seem too distracted when talking to an administrator or parent, they might not build a good rapport as needed.

Generation Y teachers are definitely the experts when it comes to technology. While Baby Boomers, and now some Generation X teachers, are considered experts in teaching because of their experience, they can learn from Generation Y regarding technology and how to implement it into their teaching. This ultimately creates a more equal teaching staff because one teacher's strength benefits another teacher's weakness. "Because N-Gen children are born with technology, they assimilate it" (Tapscott, 1998, p. 40). Generation Y isn't "afraid" of trying something new related to technology because they do not know a world without it. They have spent their lives multitasking and problem solving in order to learn about a new technology. They tend to think more analytically in the format of how a computer functions because of doing it their whole lives. This also makes them great problem solvers for when technology goes awry.

ADMINISTRATOR COMMUNICATION

Most veteran administrators are from the Baby Boomer generation, while most newer administrators are from Generation X. Administrators from both generations must understand the characteristics of newly hired Generation Y teachers and how to best assimilate them into schools. Communication between administrators and teachers is crucial, and understanding the differences in communication with Generation Y will help all administrators to effectively communicate with these teachers. This is important, also, because Generation Y will produce administrators shortly.

First, as described, Generation Y uses e-mail a lot, and typically expects speedy responses to questions posed. An administrator who waits a couple of days to respond will most likely see another e-mail or communication point from Generation Y (and sometimes Generation X) making sure that the first e-mail was received. Generation Y is used to constant feedback and communication from parents, and they expect much the same from administrators. While they see administrators as their superiors, they are not afraid of speaking with them, and will definitely seek out assistance and support if necessary.

Administrators have probably seen steady growth in technology used in teaching over the past twenty years. However, while 98 percent of American schools are connected to the Web, only 20 percent of teachers use technology communication as part of instruction (Pletka, 2007, p. 19). What this means is that administrators will see a stronger growth in technology as Generation Y teachers are hired, replacing Baby Boomer retirees. These teachers will also, typically, make choices about whom they communicate with because technology offers those choices. In other words, time and place is not a major issue hindering where they can find answers through technological communication (Pletka, 2007, p. 26). For example, instead of asking a teacher in the building a question about a science project, a teacher may chat with a teacher in another state or country about that particular science question.

However, one important area related to technology that needs to be addressed as more and more teachers use technology in teaching is that of an "Acceptable Use Policy" for various technologies available and expected in the school. Teachers must understand what is appropriate for teaching purposes, and following a guideline set forth by the school or district can help ensure everyone uses technology in a professional manner.

Another important aspect for administrators to understand is that the first children from Generation Y are now parents of small children. If a Generation Y individual was born in 1980, then it is quite conceivable that he has a child in kindergarten this year! Thus, administrators, while understanding characteristics of Generation Y for hiring teachers, are also benefiting their own understanding of Generation Y parents. These parents, like the teachers, prefer e-mail over telephoning and like the flexibility offered in current communication styles. They also often prefer e-mail messages over notes sent home, Web sites over newsletters coming home in folders, and they want to sign up for everything from volunteering in the school to ordering school supplies online. Just like Generation Y teachers, they prefer constant communication and involvement in their children's lives, and they see technology as a way to enhance home-school communication.

Administrators must keep in mind what one educator stated so well: Generation Y "lives and operates with ICT [Information Communication Technology] as habitually and automatically as I flip the light switch at my house" (Pletka, 2007, p. 35)

SUMMARY

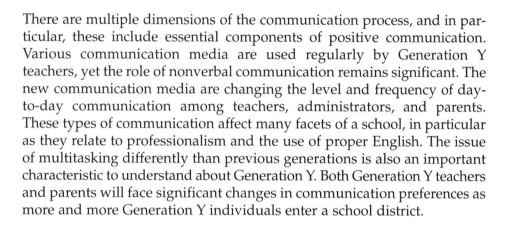

There are multiple dimensions of the communication process, and in particular, these include essential components of positive communication. Various communication media are used regularly by Generation Y teachers, yet the role of nonverbal communication remains significant. The new communication media are changing the level and frequency of day-to-day communication among teachers, administrators, and parents. These types of communication affect many facets of a school, in particular as they relate to professionalism and the use of proper English. The issue of multitasking differently than previous generations is also an important characteristic to understand about Generation Y. Both Generation Y teachers and parents will face significant changes in communication preferences as more and more Generation Y individuals enter a school district.

CASE STUDY A

Dr. Strickland is a principal of a local high school outside New York City. This high school has technology available for all teachers if they decide to use it. There has been no strong initiative for teachers to use technology, but if they want to incorporate it into their teaching, they are supported with equipment and training. The only mandatory technology initiative is e-mail. All teachers have a school e-mail address, and all teachers are expected to check e-mail at least once a day for both internal announcements and external e-mails from students or parents. Most staff issues and meetings are announced via e-mail.

Dr. Strickland sends an e-mail about an unplanned staff meeting to be held Friday after school, of the current week, because of an emergency regarding test times. The times for a particular standardized test for the school have been moved ahead two weeks from the planned time. Dr. Strickland wants to brainstorm with teachers about how to prepare the students for the tests and rearrange some of the school schedule to accommodate the date changes. One teacher, Ms. Green, e-mails Dr. Strickland back stating that she thinks it's unacceptable to call a meeting at such short notice—in particular on a Friday afternoon as she already has plans after-school. Dr. Strickland e-mails back to state that she understands her concerns, but that it is crucial that Ms. Green be there if at all possible. Ms. Green gets a bit angry with this because she will need to cancel her plans for the evening, as she won't get the train into the city in time for the event she has scheduled. She sends a very inappropriate e-mail to the principal and threatens to call her local teacher's union representative. Dr. Strickland replies to this e-mail, accidentally hitting "Reply All" which linked all teachers onto the last e-mail, stating that she is not threatened by the teacher's union. The entire string of e-mails goes to each teacher in the building.

Analyze the scenario described above by answering the following questions:

- When should Dr. Strickland have stopped the e-mail chain and gone to speak directly to Ms. Green?
- What will Dr. Strickland do now that each teacher in her building has seen the entire string of e-mails?
- What will Dr. Strickland need to do if one of the teachers forwards the e-mail onto the union representative?
- What "Acceptable Use Policy" guidelines should be put into place for intraoffice e-mail communication?
- How will Dr. Strickland approach Ms. Green now?
- What overall communication aspects were weakened because of this mishap?
- Should Dr. Strickland send an apology e-mail out to the entire staff?

CASE STUDY B

Mr. Thomas is a new Generation Y principal at an elementary school in an affluent neighborhood outside Chicago. He had a reputation for being a great first-grade teacher for five years, and when his principal retired, Mr. Thomas moved into the position. This is his first leadership position. At the start of the school year, Mr. Thomas seems very distracted by all the new things facing him. During the first two days of school, he has major issues with bussing. Many students arrive home very late, and on the second day, some students get stranded on a bus. When some parents call the school wondering where their child is, he tells them to come to school and pick their children up, and once they start arriving, he realizes that the bus driver put the children on another bus and started driving the route to drop them off; yet their parents are not home and are at school instead which means the students cannot get off the bus! Other parents are left standing at their bus stops for over thirty minutes wondering what is going on.

Understandably, some of the parents are quite upset at coming to school only to find out their children are on the bus. Many are worried about their young children getting off the bus. When some of the parents question Mr. Thomas about why this happened, he looks away, with his hands in his pocket and mumbles something that no one understands. When pressed further, he states that he has to go back inside to his office to sort out another crisis. He tells his secretary to take the names and phone numbers of the parents involved, and that he will contact them later.

Analyze the scenario described above by answering the following questions:

- What nonverbal communication issues are problematic for Mr. Thomas?
- What communication skills are lacking in this situation?
- What forum of communication would have been best for all parents of the broken-down bus, and what should Mr. Thomas do with the list of parents and their phone numbers?
- What will Mr. Thomas need to do to improve his communication skills and reputation?
- What types of technologies could help in this situation, both with the bus driver and the parents?

EXERCISE

In order to help you understand the importance of nonverbal communication in an administration role, there is a checklist below. Read each statement, and analyze whether you do it all the time, sometimes, or never. Next, evaluate each statement as to how you can modify your nonverbal communication to enhance your communication skills.

1. I look others in the eyes when speaking to them.

   _____All the time _____Sometimes _____Never

   Modification suggestions for myself _____

   _____

2. I firmly shake hands when meeting teachers and parents for the first time.

   _____All the time _____Sometimes _____Never

   Modification suggestions for myself _____

   _____

3. I use hand gestures appropriately when expressing myself.

   _____All the time _____Sometimes _____Never

   Modification suggestions for myself _____

   _____

4. My office looks inviting and welcoming from the way the furniture is arranged and what decorates the walls.

_____All the time _____Sometimes _____Never

Modification suggestions for myself _____

_____

5. I look directly at the person I'm speaking to (rather than looking around at distractions) as well as when they respond to show that I am listening attentively.

_____All the time _____Sometimes _____Never

Modification suggestions for myself _____

_____

6. I smile regularly at staff and students as I walk through school buildings.

_____All the time _____Sometimes _____Never

Modification suggestions for myself _____

_____

7. I use appropriate facial expressions as I encounter situations such as children laughing in the hallway or children fighting in the hallway.

_____All the time _____Sometimes _____Never

Modification suggestions for myself _____

_____

8. I choose my dress particularly for the impression I want to create for myself.

_____All the time _____Sometimes _____Never

Modification suggestions for myself _____

_____

9. I stand tall and avoid fidgeting when interacting with parents and teachers.

_____All the time _____Sometimes _____Never

Modification suggestions for myself _____

_____

10. I nod as I listen to others to show that I am paying attention to what they are saying.

_____All the time _____Sometimes _____Never

Modification suggestions for myself _____

_____

CHAPTER FOCUS QUESTIONS

1. Explain the various types of nonverbal communication and how these may change the outcome of a conversation.

2. Provide an example or scenario where a Generation Y teacher's informal use of English in an e-mail might worry a parent or administrator.

3. If you, as an administrator, were presenting a new curriculum to your faculty and saw two new Generation Y teachers at the back talking and typing on their laptops, what would you do?

4. Provide an example of a topic of conversation that should happen face-to-face instead of in an e-mail exchange.

5. List some of the technology communication media that are available to teachers at your school. Which teachers use these regularly? What generation are they from?

Hiring and Compensating Generation Y Teachers and Administrators

CHAPTER OBJECTIVES

The following objectives are the focus of this chapter:

- To hire Generation Y administrators and teachers who will be successful

- To have the right number of Generation Y teachers and administrators with the right skills, in the right place, and at the right time in order to fulfill the mission and vision of a given school and school district

- To hire Generation Y teachers and administrators who will support, through their professional activities, the intellectual, emotional, physical, and ethical development of students

- To develop intrinsic and extrinsic reward programs that attract and retain Generation Y teachers and administrators

- To develop salary and fringe benefits programs that will attract and retain Generation Y teachers and administrators

VIGNETTE

As a student, Ms. Otto was always very happy and determined. She worked hard her whole life, and was excited to become a teacher. She got married during her junior year of college, and wanted to start a family right away. However, she was also determined to have a successful teaching career. Therefore, she decided to plan her first pregnancy during her senior year. Her baby was due in late May, and she was excited to then hopefully start a new teaching job that August. She realized that she would need to apply and interview for jobs while pregnant, but she did not think this be an issue since she would have her baby long before her new job began. Also, as a Generation Y student, and one who recently finished coursework including the course titled "School Law," she knew that there could be legal ramifications if the interview committees of any school questioned her about pregnancy. She also had been utilizing the career services and counseling departments at her university for strategies to use during interviewing. One career counselor said that while interviewing, some teachers or administrators may comment positively about the pregnancy by asking questions such as, "When are you due?" or "How has your pregnancy been?" But, she thought they probably would not say anything.

During her first interview, Ms. Otto was shocked when the interviewers asked about her pregnancy and how that may impact her as a new teacher. She quickly and calmly reminded the interview panel that this was a question outside of legally accepted boundaries, and that she could focus instead on explaining how she would be an effective teacher in their school.

CHARACTERISTICS OF GENERATION Y

Generation Y teachers and principals are like other generations in terms of wanting to be justly compensated for their work. However, Generation Y teachers and administrators seem to more often articulate their desire to find purposefulness in their careers. This does not imply that Generation Y teachers and administrators are significantly different than teachers and administrators from other generations, but rather, Generation Y has an intensity of wanting their work activities to be explicitly purposeful. This presents somewhat of a challenge because in educating children, it is often difficult to see meaningful progress within the immediate future (Half, 2008; Lovely & Buffum, 2007).

As employees of a school district, Generation Y teachers and administrators definitely want financial rewards for their performance and place a high value on salary and fringe benefits. They also know and understand their rights and how people are treated differently across districts. Thus, they tend to include working conditions along with salaries and benefits when making comparisons to teachers and administrators in other school districts. If the opportunity arises, they may well be prepared to apply for positions in those wealthier school districts. Salary and fringe benefits can be considered symbolic of the value that a school district has for its employees. Fringe benefits that are most desired are medical, hospitalization, dental, life insurance, and tuition reimbursement (Half, 2008; Lovely & Buffum, 2007).

SELECTING AND HIRING GENERATION Y TEACHERS AND ADMINISTRATORS

A selection decision may result in four possible outcomes, two being correct decisions and two being errors. The correct decisions occur when the individual hired proves to be successful on the job or when a rejected applicant would have performed inadequately if hired. In both instances, the selection process has met the objective of hiring the most appropriate candidate (Rebore, 2007). The process has failed when a rejected candidate could have performed successfully on the job or when the individual hired performs inadequately (Young, 2008, pp. 129–131).

Developing the Job Descriptions for Generation Y Applicants

A written job description is the end product of a process that is commonly referred to as "job analysis." This process gathers information about the position: what an employee does; why he or she performs certain tasks; how he or she does the job; what skills, education, or training are required to perform the job; the relationship the job has to other jobs; and the physical demands and environmental conditions that affect the job. This information also is relevant to human resources forecasting, to creating job evaluation instruments, and in determining compensation programs.

A number of recognized techniques can be used in job analysis. These include observations, individual interviews, group interviews, job questionnaires, employee ratings, expert consulting, supervisor analysis, and the diary method.

No one format for writing a job description can be universally acclaimed as most effective in each and every circumstance. However, certain elements should be common to most job descriptions. These include the title of the job, duties that must be performed, the authority and responsibilities accompanying the job, and specific qualifications necessary for successful performance of the job. Each description begins with a summary of the job that outlines the overall responsibilities of the position. This is followed by a detailed explanation of specific job tasks and the relationship of the job to other positions in the organizational structure of the school district. At a time when legal rights and responsibilities are being emphasized by parents and employees, organizational relationships are extremely important and must be clearly explained to prospective employees. Finally, minimum job qualifications should be listed as an integral part of the job description.

Developing Selection Criteria for Generation Y Applicants

The second step in the selection procedure is to establish the criteria against which the candidates will be evaluated to determine who will be offered the job. Selection criteria are very different from the job description, in that the selection criteria delineate those ideal characteristics that, if possessed by an individual to the fullest extent possible, would ensure the successful performance of the job. Obviously, no one person will possess all the characteristics to the fullest extent, and not all characteristics have equal importance in determining who the best candidate is. The use of selection criteria can also become a method for quantifying the expert opinions of those who will interview candidates. Without criteria, interviewers are left to their own, individual, discretion in determining if an individual will be able to perform the job.

Quantifying the opinions of interviewers also provides data to show that the best candidate was offered the position, thus demonstrating that the school district is an affirmative action and equal opportunity employer. The candidate with the highest score should be offered the position first; if he or she does not accept, then the candidate receiving the next highest score should be offered the position, and so on.

The timing for writing the job description and for developing the selection criteria is extremely important. Both tasks should be performed before a job vacancy is advertised and before applications are received, not only because the advertisement should be based on the description, but also because it will demonstrate that the criteria were not prepared to favor any particular applicant (Young & Castetter, 2003, pp. 106–108).

Writing Job Vacancy Announcements and Advertising Positions for Generation Y Applicants

The advertisement should be viewed as an integral part of the selection process. It is based on the job description and should provide potential candidates with sufficient information to make a decision on whether to apply for the position. Consequently, an advertisement must clearly identify the job title, major responsibilities of the job, the name and location of the school district, how to apply for the job, and the minimum qualifications to become a candidate. A common mistake made by some administrators and inexperienced human resources administrators is not allotting sufficient time to effectively implement the selection process. A hurried process may place the school district in an indefensible position in terms of affirmative action requirements and, in addition, may result in the hiring of the wrong person.

Receiving Applications and Selecting Generation Y Candidates to Be Interviewed

A central-office staff member, usually a secretary, should be assigned to receive all the applications for a given job vacancy. As the applications are received, they should be dated and placed in a designated file folder. This will provide integrity to the process, and also will provide a method of monitoring the incoming applications for a particular vacancy.

Many applicants will make requests to their college or university placement offices to send their transcripts and letters of reference to the school district. These documents must also be dated and attached to the appropriate applications. After the deadline for receiving applications has been reached, a master list should be compiled with the names, addresses, and telephone numbers of those who have applied. The master list also should include, by title, the other documents that have been received in support of each application, such as transcripts and letters of reference. The entire folder of applications, support documents, and the master list can then be assigned and given to a human resources administrator who will perform the initial screening of the applications. Alternatively, these can be housed in a secure online environment with access allowed by only those designated.

Keeping applicants informed during the selection process will help cut down on the number of inquiries that are normally received in the human resources department. One very effective method is to send a postcard or e-mail message to each applicant stating that the application has been received and listing the date by which individuals will be selected for interviews.

It is also important to immediately notify those who sent in applications after the deadline that they will not be considered for the position. A common practice is to accept those applications postmarked or received electronically on the day of the deadline. Some school districts and many colleges and universities have initiated the practice of receiving applications on a rolling basis until the position is filled. Under this procedure, individuals who sent their applications to the school district by the deadline are given first consideration. If a suitable candidate is not identified, then those individuals who sent their applications to the district before a later designated date are considered, and so on, until a suitable candidate is offered and accepts the position. This is an acceptable practice that can encourage qualified individuals to apply for positions even when they did not know about the positions in a timely manner (Webb & Norton, 2009, pp. 113–121).

Screening the applications is the fifth step in the selection process. It is initiated to identify those applicants who are to be interviewed for the position. The application form should contain a statement requesting the applicants to have their placement papers, transcripts, and letters of reference sent to the human resources department. These documents, along with the application form, will provide the human resources administrator with sufficient information to evaluate each person against the selection criteria and against the minimum education and certification requirements.

The number of applicants to be interviewed will depend on the number of people who apply and on the nature of the position to be filled. If only five people apply for a vacancy and if each person meets the minimum qualifications, all five can be interviewed. This, of course, is not the norm except for those very few job classifications in which there is a shortage of qualified individuals, such as the field of special education. On average, between three and five applicants are selected to be interviewed for teaching positions. For school executive positions, the average number interviewed is between five and ten applicants.

INTERVIEWING GENERATION Y CANDIDATES

Interviewing candidates is a responsibility shared between the human resources department and other school district employees. The individuals who will participate in the interviewing process will be determined by the position to be filled. It is important to include not only those who will supervise the new employee, but also others who have expert knowledge about the duties to be performed by the successful candidate. For example, candidates for a high school biology teaching position should be interviewed by the high school principal, the chairperson of the biology department, a biology teacher, a human resources administrator, and the assistant superintendent for secondary education. In like manner, candidates for an elementary principal position should be interviewed by the superintendent of schools, the assistant superintendent for elementary education, an elementary school principal, and a human resources administrator (Webb & Norton, 2009).

Members of the interviewing committee will need assistance in learning the strategies for credential evaluation and interviewing. A method that will hold down expenses and make maximum use of the skills learned through a staff development program is to select a group of Generation Y teachers, department chairpersons, classified employees, and building principals who will participate in the selection process for a year's time. Each year, a different group of employees can be selected and trained to participate in evaluating credentials and interviewing applicants (Webb & Norton, 2009).

Essentially, an interview is a conversation between two individuals set up to generate information about the person being interviewed or other matters that are familiar to the respondent. However, there are four characteristics of an interview that distinguish it from an ordinary conversation. First, an interview is a structured conversation with direction and a format; it has a beginning, middle, and conclusion. Second, the interview is conducted by an individual who is prepared to move it in a direction dictated by the occasion. Third, both parties to the interview understand its purpose, which can be accomplished only through cooperation. Finally, the nature of the interview is clearly defined and specified (Webb & Norton, 2009).

There are two basic types of interviews, the standardized interview and the open-ended interview. The standardized interview is conducted by asking a set of questions established to help ensure that the responses of the candidates can be readily compared. It is most effective in the initial interviewing of all candidates.

The open-ended interview encourages the candidate to talk freely and at length about topics introduced by the interviewer to suit the occasion. It is very helpful in the follow-up sessions with the finalists for the job. In both types of interviews, the objectives are basically the same. The interviewer is attempting to gather facts from the respondent—to learn about the respondent's opinions, beliefs, and attitudes; and to experience the respondent as a person (Webb & Norton, 2009).

The interviewer has extremely important responsibilities. Along with directing the interview by asking questions, the interviewer must also record the respondent's answers and present the respondent with a favorable image of the school district. Through the interview process, the interviewers must evaluate and come to a conclusion about the suitability of each candidate. A selection criteria instrument should be used to quantify the observations of the interviewer, but ultimately the observations are subjective interpretations (Webb & Norton, 2009).

All interviews are more effective if they are conducted in a pleasant environment. This will help put the candidate at ease and will facilitate the kind of verbal exchange that gives the interviewer the most information about each candidate. The interviewer should find a room that allows the interview to be conducted without interruptions and should arrange the furniture in the room so as to have eye contact with the candidate throughout the session (Webb & Norton, 2009).

Federal legislation and court decisions have had a significant impact on the types of questions that legally may be asked in an interview. For example, it was once common practice to ask candidates if they had ever been arrested or spent time in jail. Because of a court case, *Gregory v. Litton Systems, Inc.,* school districts are now permitted to ask only about a candidate's record of criminal conviction. Further, questions about sexual preference are prohibited under antidiscrimination laws. Generation Y candidates, in particular, know and understand their rights (Webb & Norton, 2009).

The success of the entire interviewing process rests on the interviewer's skill in asking questions. It is a skill that is acquired through experience. However, a well-planned interview with a predetermined set of questions can be extremely useful to even the most experienced interviewer, and it is a necessity in the standardized interview (Webb & Norton, 2009).

Some school districts prefer group interviewing, in which a number of staff members who are scheduled to interview a candidate jointly perform this task. Group interviewing can be very effective, and it certainly cuts down on the amount of time spent on this process. The dynamics described in this chapter are also applicable to the group interviewing method. However, to be effective, one staff member must serve as the group leader and take responsibility for directing the interview (Webb & Norton, 2009).

Checking references and credentials, the seventh step in the selection process, has profound implications. A candidate's "credentials" include such items as a college or university transcript, administrator or teacher certification documents, and a physician's verification of health. Transcripts and health verifications should not be accepted if they are presented to the human resources department by the applicant; rather, they should be mailed directly to the school district by the respective college or university and physician. It is important to inform candidates that their files are not complete until these documents are received (Webb & Norton, 2009).

It is common and accepted practice to request the health verification from a candidate only if the applicant is chosen for the position. However, a contract of formal employment should not be initiated until the health verification has been received in the human resources department. It is best to state on the application form that a health examination will be required as a condition of employment if a job offer is made (Webb & Norton, 2009).

An administrator or teacher certification document is usually issued by a state department of education and given directly to the individual. Although the candidate presents the certification document to the human resources department, it is still necessary to contact the issuing state in order to ascertain if the certification remains valid. When a certification is revoked, the actual document is not always returned by the individual to the state department of education (Webb & Norton, 2009).

The risk of hiring a person who has a criminal record has created much concern for human resources administrators. School districts have been sensitized to this possibility because of the news media notoriety given to educators who have been convicted of child molestation. This is probably the ultimate nightmare for every school administrator. Criminal background investigations are time-consuming and expensive, in addition to being controversial. The National Education Association has taken a position in opposition to fingerprinting as a condition of employment. However, many school districts require the fingerprinting of potential employees as part of a background investigation conducted through law enforcement agencies (Webb & Norton, 2009).

The conducting of criminal background investigations and the extent of such investigations is usually dependent upon a mix of school district policy, state statutes, and the discretion of the interviewing human resources administrator. The extent of the investigation is usually limited in most school districts to checking with the local and state police in order to ascertain if the potential employee has been convicted of a crime. If the candidate is a teacher, it is also possible to check with the Teacher Identification Clearinghouse, which is maintained by the National Association of State Directors of Teacher Education and Certification (NASDTEC). This nationwide clearinghouse has a database of all teachers who have been denied certification and whose certification has been revoked or suspended for moral reasons. The data is available only to states that have joined the Clearinghouse. Individual school districts can neither join the Clearinghouse nor directly obtain information from it. Only states may join (Garvey, 2001, pp. 95–104).

Selecting the Best Generation Y Candidate and Making the Job Offer

The human resources administrator responsible for implementing the selection process for a particular vacancy must organize all relevant data in such a manner that a choice may eventually be made by the superintendent of schools. The data should include the rank ordering by scores against the selection criteria of those candidates who were interviewed, verified credentials and reference letters, and the application forms. The superintendent then selects the candidate who appears best qualified. If this selection process is utilized, this will usually be the candidate who scored the highest against the selection criteria.

The superintendent of schools may wish to interview the candidate selected for a position or may wish to interview the top two to five candidates before making a final choice. When the final decision has been made, the selected candidate must be offered the job in a formal manner. If this individual accepts the offer, a contract must be approved by the board of education and signed by the finalist. Usually, a board of education will require the superintendent to make a recommendation of employment and will want an explanation of why this particular person was selected.

COMPENSATING GENERATION Y TEACHERS AND ADMINISTRATORS

The Psychology of Compensating Generation Y Candidates

Before engaging in any activity, every human being consciously or subconsciously asks the same question, "What will I get out of this?" Psychologists have recognized for a long time that satisfaction of needs is the motivation behind all actions. This satisfaction or reward might be money, a promotion, recognition, acceptance, receipt of information, or the feeling that comes from doing a good job (Babcock, 2005, pp. 50–57).

From an administrative standpoint, managers can develop a unique compensation system if they understand what their teachers and administrators believe to be in their best interest. Not all individuals value the same type of compensation. Consequently, a compensation program must be flexible enough to meet the expectations of individual employees. It is also necessary to structure a compensation program in such a way that people realize they are acting in their own best interest when they are acting in the best interest of the school district. This exemplifies the importance of compensation in an "expectancy model." As a result of this model, several things become clear.

Compensation must be linked to behaviors that the school system classifies as desirable. The employee should recognize that good job performance is compatible with self-interest. Employees should recognize that the compensation system also will satisfy their own needs; therefore, administrators must analyze and interpret the needs of the employees. The most obvious way to learn about an individual's needs is to ask the person.

Issues Affecting Compensation of Generation Y Teachers and Administrators

The main purpose for establishing a compensation policy is to attract and retain qualified employees who will provide the type of service expected by the public. It is essential that employees understand the compensation structure and have confidence in the objectivity by which the system is implemented. Five major variables must be taken into consideration by the administration when constructing and recommending a compensation policy to the board of education for approval: performance, effort, seniority, skills, and job requirements.

The evaluation of performance is concerned with a basic question: did you get the job done? Compensating individuals requires criteria that define performance. The importance of using performance as a basis for compensating employees is critical to all effective compensation systems.

School districts have required teachers to consider the effort put forth by students as a determinant in evaluating student performance. Even if effort does not directly influence a grade, some method is usually employed to indicate whether a given student is putting forth her best effort. It is ironic, therefore, that school districts have long neglected using the degree of effort put forth by employees as a component in their compensation systems. Yet, without such an orientation, a school district will fall prey to compensating quantity rather than quality and the end rather than the means. Also, there are some situations when an outcome is difficult to evaluate and effort becomes a primary determinant of compensation.

This discussion is concerned with a topic much debated in education: performance incentives. There is no one best method for rewarding performance with money; however, the following comments will help to clarify this issue. If compensation is to motivate performance, employees must recognize the relationship between performance and compensation. Most school districts have traditionally used nonperformance criteria, such as seniority-based salary schedules, for allocating compensation. However, this chapter views compensation primarily as a payoff for performance. This concept is in keeping with the outcry for accountability and, if properly applied, might be the only realistic approach to improving the quality of education. For too long, teachers and other employees of school districts have been placed apart from the rest of mankind by taxpayers who believe that they should be more dedicated to service than concerned about making a living. Teachers and other public employees have fought this long-held belief by engaging in unionism and collective negotiations for wages and fringe benefits. A reasonable compensation system, recognizing quality performance and objectively administered, could help remedy some of the dissatisfaction voiced by school district employees (Cunningham & Cordeiro, 2000, p. 307).

The most obvious kinds of compensation are wages and fringe benefits. However, a truly effective compensation system must be multifaceted, incorporating both intrinsic and extrinsic aspects. Although modern school districts employ people in many different occupational categories, many of the possible rewards are applicable only to particular job positions. In addition, rewarding performance and encouraging higher levels of performance must be fashioned into a comprehensive system that is ongoing and integral to the operation of the school district.

Intrinsic rewards are those that an employee receives from doing the job itself. The employee's satisfaction on the job is usually increased by the following: participation in the policy-making process, greater job discretion, increased responsibility, and opportunities for professional development.

Extrinsic rewards are divided into direct and indirect compensation. The most common forms of direct compensation are salary, overtime pay, holiday pay, and merit pay for performance. Direct compensation is also the part of a compensation system that generates the most controversy and disgruntlement among employees. Industrial psychologists have long contended that rate of pay is not the most important determinant of job satisfaction. However, it is an indispensable part of every compensation package and, because of its importance, is treated at length in a separate section in this chapter. Indirect compensation usually includes insurance programs, pay for time away from work, and services. There is a widespread attitude among human resources administrators to view indirect compensation as that which helps to retain individuals in an organization rather than motivate them to greater performance. Direct compensation is considered the stimulus to better performance. Because of the complexity and importance of indirect compensation, more frequently referred to as fringe benefits, this also is addressed in a separate section in this chapter.

Nonfinancial rewards have begun to appear in some school districts. These rewards may either motivate employees to greater performance or help to retain their services. The limits to the kind and extent of nonfinancial compensation are established only by the creativity of those responsible for establishing a compensation program. Nonfinancial compensation, however, is effective only if it meets the needs of specific employees. What one person considers desirable might seem superfluous to another. For example, a very status-conscious employee might be motivated by a job title, a reserved parking place, the services of a private secretary, or a paneled and carpeted office. Another individual might value working without close supervision that could both motivate performance and retain his services. The significant point is that organizations can use a variety of nonfinancial means as part of a total program and that these means may be more appreciated by certain individuals than direct or indirect forms of compensation. Generation Y teachers and administrators would consider incentive pay tied to their performance as affirmation of their success.

However, it is also important to develop both internal and external rewards, with nonfinancial rewards adding to the overall attempt to hire and retain Generation Y teachers and administrators.

The Effects of Salary on Motivating
Generation Y Teachers and Administrators

An interesting question central to all pay systems is, "Does money stimulate an employee to put forth more effort?" The answer to this question is closely related to individual needs, because money in itself is rarely an end but rather a means to "purchasing an end." A $4,000 raise for an employee making $40,000 a year would help that individual maintain the standard of living in the face of ordinary inflation. That same raise would considerably improve the standard of living for an individual earning $20,000 a year, but it would have much less effect on the lifestyle of someone earning $80,000 per year. From this perspective, money does have a potential to motivate if individuals are seeking to maintain or improve their standard of living. It is rare to find a person who is not concerned when her lifestyle deteriorates because salary increases have not kept pace with inflation. If money is to motivate an individual within an organization to greater performance, it must be very clear that such performance is indeed rewarded with more money. The behavior that is thus rewarded will be repeated, and the behaviors that are not rewarded with money will be extinguished. In addition to this experientially proven conclusion, statistical data support the position that money increases intrinsic motivation under the following two conditions: (1) monetary rewards must closely follow performance so as to be reinforcing, and (2) the employee must perceive the monetary rewards as being related to work behavior.

Compensation Packages for
Generation Y Teachers and Administrators

Because individual employees have individual needs, no compensation program will satisfy every employee. A number of corporations, recognizing this fact, have developed compensation programs commonly referred to as "cafeteria" plans, which allow each employee to choose the combination of programs most attractive to that person. Thus, employees are informed that their compensation is a certain dollar amount, and they then choose a mix of salary and other benefits suited to their particular situation and offered by the corporation. Such benefits might include: major medical and hospitalization insurance, pharmaceutical insurance, dental insurance, optical insurance, flexible spending plans, life insurance, extended care insurance, dependent care plans, accidental death and dismemberment insurance, long-term disability insurance, travel accident insurance, adoption assistance, and annuities.

Equity of Pay for Generation Y Teachers and Administrators

In any organization, employees tend to compare what they get from their jobs with what they must put into their work. At the same time, they are comparing what they make in wages with what coworkers make and how productive their coworkers are. The inevitable outcome of this comparison process is that individual will see their compensation as either equal or unequal to that of fellow employees. Those who feel inequality exists will view themselves as underrewarded or overrewarded.

Equity of pay continues to be a concern of the Equal Employment Opportunity Commission as they receive allegations each year from females stating that they are being paid less than their male counterparts. All inequalities in pay are violations of the Equal Pay Act of 1963 and Title VII of the Civil Rights Act of 1964 (Stites, 2005, pp. 65–69).

FRINGE BENEFIT PROGRAMS FOR GENERATION Y TEACHERS AND ADMINISTRATORS

Fringe benefits are defined as benefits available to all employees resulting from a direct fiscal expenditure. Because fringe benefits are available to all employees and are not contingent upon performance, such services are not motivators, but are more properly considered maintenance factors. Nevertheless, fringe benefits are commonly considered to be an important part of an effective compensation program. Retirement programs, medical and hospitalization insurance, and life insurance are only a few of the many fringe benefits offered to employees in school systems. Because these services are essential in our society, the quality of these and other fringe benefit programs can have a significant effect on the ability of a school district to attract and retain good employees. Conversely, absenteeism and employee turnover, which are signs of employee dissatisfaction, can possibly be kept to a tolerable level with good fringe benefit and salary programs. High employee turnover across the nation costs school districts millions of dollars each year. Recruiting, and hiring new employees, which creates direct expenditures of money, should be minimized to a reasonable turnover rate. This factor, however, does not begin to address the problem of meeting the primary objective of the school district to educate students when there is a continual flow of new employees.

The cost of fringe benefits in the United States has risen to approximately 35 percent of total salary and wages paid to employees. School districts across the country are experiencing severe financial problems. With financial problems continuing to spread, school districts have found that fringe benefit enrichment is an alternative when large wage and salary increases are not feasible. As more school districts develop elaborate fringe benefit programs, greater pressure is being placed on competing school districts to develop similar programs to attract and keep employees.

There is also a growing recognition that fringe benefits are nontaxable, which has been another major stimulus toward their expansion. If a teacher wants a certain amount of life insurance, there are two advantages in having it purchased by the school district. First, the premium will be lower because the school district will be purchasing a large degree of protection. Second, the teacher would pay the premium for the insurance out of his gross pay, which is the dollar amount before paying taxes. If the school district pays the premium, the teacher has more wages left to pay for other needs and, therefore, this becomes an attractive fringe benefit.

Certain benefits must be provided by the school district: social security premiums, state retirement insurance, unemployment compensation, and workers' compensation. These benefits provide the employee with financial security and protection at retirement or termination, or when an injury occurs in the workplace; they also provide survivors' benefits to dependents in the event of the employee's death.

The social security program usually covers classified employees. Instructional and administrative personnel are normally included in state retirement programs. Social security is the major source of income for U.S. retirees. This program is financed by the contributions of employees, which are matched by the employer and computed as a percentage of the employee's earnings. Survivors' benefits for the dependents of a deceased employee and disability benefits for an employee who is unable to be gainfully employed are provided through the social security administration.

The Social Security Act is an important aspect of the United States government's attempt to care for and protect the aged by ensuring a minimal standard of living for them. Although social security is often referred to as an insurance program, this is a misnomer. Rather, it is a transfer program of a trust fund from one generation to another. We, the currently employed, pay a social security tax that is used to support yesterday's retired workers, dependents, and the disabled. It is important for human resources administrators to be cognizant of the fact that social security benefits and the program itself are subject to legislation. Thus, changes are certain to occur and must be continually monitored to ensure that adequate budgetary appropriations are available to meet the demands of these potential changes.

Unemployment compensation laws in most states provide benefits to individuals who are without a job. To qualify for these benefits, a person usually submits an application to the state employment agency for unemployment benefits and registers with that agency, willing to accept suitable employment offered through the agency. In addition, the person must have worked a minimum number of weeks before becoming unemployed. Unemployment benefits are derived from a tax levied against employers calculated on a percentage of the employer's total salary payroll. Benefits received by unemployed workers are calculated from the individual's previous wage rate plus the length of previous employment. Unemployment benefits are provided on a limited basis, typically for a twenty-six week period. Unemployment compensation also serves the total economy of our nation because it provides stability in spending power during periods of high unemployment, as when a recession occurs.

Workers' compensation programs provide benefits to individuals injured or disabled while engaged in a job-related activity. Benefits paid to employees for injuries are based on schedules for minimum and maximum payments, depending on the type of injury sustained. For example, the loss of a hand is compensated with a higher dollar amount than the loss of a finger. In like manner, disability payments are calculated based on the individual's current salary, future earnings, and financial responsibilities. The funds for workers' compensation programs are borne entirely by the employer. Although the programs are mandated by state laws, the method of obtaining workers' compensation insurance is usually left to the discretion of the employer, who may buy such protection from public or private agencies or provide the protection through a self-insuring program. Like social security and unemployment insurance, workers' compensation is subject to the legislative process. Thus, requirements and benefits will certainly change with the passage of time.

Where mandated by state laws, retirement programs for administrators and teachers generally follow the prescriptions of these other protection programs. Contributions are calculated on the basis of an employee's wages and are usually matched by the school district. Benefits based on contributions are paid upon retirement, with survivors' benefits being available for the dependents of deceased employees.

In 1986, the United States Congress passed the Consolidated Omnibus Budget Reconciliation Act (COBRA). This federal law requires employers that provide group health plans for their employees and their dependents to offer an extension of the coverage on a temporary basis under certain conditions when coverage would usually end. An employee covered by the group health plan is eligible for continuation of coverage if his or her employment is terminated, except in cases of gross misconduct. Examples of situations where an individual would be eligible for continuation of coverage include being laid off for economic reasons or being reduced to part-time employment and thereby normally losing coverage.

Family members of an employee are entitled to continued coverage under the following qualifying events: death of the employee; divorce or legal separation from the employee; Medicare becoming the employee's primary healthcare coverage; termination, layoff, or part-time status of the employee; and ceasing to be considered a dependent under the plan. There are notification requirements under this law and the employee or family members must pay the premiums for the extended group health plan coverage. Extended coverage may last for eighteen, twenty-nine, or thirty-six months depending on certain qualifying conditions.

There are also voluntary benefits that are further divided into insurance programs, time away from the job, and services. Group insurance programs are available for almost every human need. Among the most common are major medical and hospitalization insurance, dental insurance, term life insurance, errors and omissions insurance, and optical insurance. The number of such programs made available to employees depends on the fiscal condition of the school district and the wishes of the employees. A school district is usually restricted by state statute to paying insurance premiums only for employees. Therefore, an employee who wishes to include dependents under such insurance programs must pay the additional premium for this coverage.

Under federal law and Internal Revenue Service regulations, school districts can design "cafeteria" fringe benefit plans, which will allow individual employees to choose the benefits that most meet their needs. In addition, if the employee is to bear the cost of some of these programs, the premiums paid can be deducted from the gross salary or wages before federal income taxes are levied.

This tax advantage for employees and the opportunity to choose their benefits from a predetermined list are two reasons why such programs are quite desirable. The administrative expense of such a program and the availability of insurance coverage that does not demand a high percentage of participation are problems. For example, a company may offer a dental insurance program to a school district only if there is 60 percent participation by employees.

A fringe benefit that is often taken for granted by employees, but creates an additional expense for a school district, is time spent away from work. Therefore, sick leave, vacation time, paid holidays, and sabbatical leave are, in fact, benefits provided at the discretion of the school system. In very large school districts this amounts to a considerable expenditure.

Corporations have long recognized the value of services in a fringe benefit program. Social and recreational events, employee assistance programs, wellness programs, cultural activities, credit unions, company cafeterias, company-provided transportation to and from work, tuition reimbursements, and childcare centers are only a few of the services found in many large corporations. School systems usually provide much more limited services. Services, such as time away from work, are seldom recognized by employees as fringe benefits. Those most commonly found in public education are expenses paid for attendance at workshops, professional meetings, and conventions; tuition reimbursement; and free lunches and coffee. In large school districts, central-office administrators are usually provided with district-owned automobiles to use when engaged in school business, or they receive mileage reimbursement.

This section contains a significant amount of information that is important for administrators to know as they manage the human resources assets of a school district to the benefit of all employees, including Generation Y teachers and administrators. Further, it is important for administrators to know the characteristics of Generation Y teachers and administrations set forth at the beginning of each chapter as the context within which the chapter material should be applied to Generation Y.

SUMMARY

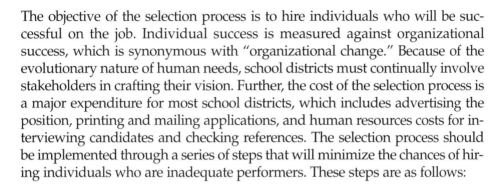

The objective of the selection process is to hire individuals who will be successful on the job. Individual success is measured against organizational success, which is synonymous with "organizational change." Because of the evolutionary nature of human needs, school districts must continually involve stakeholders in crafting their vision. Further, the cost of the selection process is a major expenditure for most school districts, which includes advertising the position, printing and mailing applications, and human resources costs for interviewing candidates and checking references. The selection process should be implemented through a series of steps that will minimize the chances of hiring individuals who are inadequate performers. These steps are as follows:

- Developing the job description for Generation Y applicants
- Developing the selection criteria for Generation Y applicants
- Writing the job vacancy announcement and advertising the position for Generation Y applicants
- Receiving applications and selecting Generation Y candidates to be interviewed
- Interviewing Generation Y candidates
- Selecting the best Generation Y candidate and making the job offer

School district administrators should attempt to utilize an "expectancy model" as the vehicle for developing a compensation system. With this model, compensation is linked to employee behaviors that both meet the objectives of the school district and satisfy the needs of the employees. Five variables must be taken into consideration in a compensation program: (1) employee performance, (2) effort, (3) seniority, (4) skills, and (5) job requirements. The rewarding of performance, however, must be the primary objective of a compensation program.

An effective program must include both intrinsic and extrinsic compensation. Intrinsic compensation consists of those that pertain to the quality of the job situation; they may include participation in the policy-making process, increased responsibility, and greater job discretion. Extrinsic rewards are divided into direct and indirect compensation. Direct compensation is commonly referred to as salary or wages; indirect compensation is frequently referred to as fringe benefits. Nonfinancial compensation has begun to appear in some school districts and is limited only by the imagination of the administration.

CASE STUDY

A school district in an affluent suburb of a medium-sized city has a standard salary scale as depicted in Table 5.1. (Step is related to the number of years in the district, BA, MA, and PhD are relevant degrees, and "+ number" includes a degree plus additional university credit hours earned.)

Table 5.1   Teachers' Salary Schedule

Step	BA	BA+15	MA	MA+15	MA+30	PhD
1	45457	46566	47675	51005	62088	75393
2	46566	47675	48784	52110	63197	77610
3	47675	48784	49892	53218	64306	79828
4	48784	49892	51001	54327	65414	82045
5	51001	52110	53218	56545	67632	84263
6	52110	53218	54327	57653	68741	86480
7	53218	54327	55436	58762	69849	88697
8	54327	57099	59871	63197	73730	92578
9	58762	63197	67077	70404	80936	96458
10	64278	69800	75324	78379	89072	101999
11	65478	71000	76524	79579	90272	103199
12	67878	73400	78924	81979	92672	105599
13	71478	77000	82524	85579	96272	109199
14	76278	81800	87324	90379	101072	113999

Ms. Kerrigan, the assistant superintendent for human resources at this district has always used a scale such as this. In fact, when she asks for details regarding the history of teacher salaries and compensation for the district, the information found shows that as far as can be traced, salaries were always defined on this level. In other words, salary in this particular district has always been affected solely by degrees earned, number of credit hours earned beyond particular degrees, and number of years served in the district. While most teachers in the district have seemed content with this scale since it is competitive in the area, Ms. Kerrigan has "heard through the grapevine" that a few neighboring districts have started to change their teacher-salary scale to be based in effort and merit instead. In fact, upon further investigation, she finds that when comparing the ages of new hires in her district over the past three years to the ages of new hires in a neighboring district over the past three years, that her new hires tend to be in the age 25 to 29 range while the others are in the age 21 to 25 range. As contracts are issued, she finds that a few newly hired Generation Y teachers in her district are leaving to take a new job at the neighboring district.

Realizing a potential problem, Ms. Kerrigan asks for exit interviews for all teachers leaving the district. What she finds out is that some are retiring, but all Generation Y teachers, Generation Y administrators, and Generation Y hopeful administrators are leaving because of the salary scale. The neighboring district's salary scale rewards effort and merit in addition to years of service and level of education. Because they want rewarding careers where they are coached to rise to the highest level possible, they want a district that will train and reward them for doing so. They have seen fellow teachers in that district earn more money for good work, and they decide they want that same opportunity.

Analyze the scenario described above by answering the following questions:

- How should Ms. Kerrigan proceed regarding this issue?
- If she decides to change the salary scale, in what ways should she modify it? What aspects of teaching and promotion should be included in the new scale?
- If she decides to change the salary scale, how will this affect Generation X and Baby Boomer teachers?
- If she decides not to change the salary scale, how will this affect attracting Generation Y teachers and administrators to the district?
- What types of fringe benefits may need to be addressed when considering the salary scale?

EXERCISES

- Your school district has been investigated by the Equal Employment Opportunity Commission because of complaints from a number of people who are members of a minority group protected by federal laws concerning the interview process. In your position as the assistant superintendent for human resources, you are meeting with the administrators, teachers, and support staff members who will be involved in the interview process to fill a number of vacancies. Write a brief explanation of the interview process, setting forth its objectives and format. Also, identify the types of questions that are appropriate and those that are not.

- Obtain a copy of the policies from a school district concerning the selection process and write a comparison of them with the process set forth in this chapter.

- Review the job descriptions for a teaching and an administrative position from a school district. Write a comparison of them with those found in this chapter.

- Review the application forms used in a school district and evaluate them in relation to the principles for application construction found in this chapter.

- Develop, in writing, a list of interview questions that you think will help identify the most qualified applicant.

- Interview a human resources administrator in person or on the telephone in order to find out how his or her school district conducts background checks.

- You are the director of employee benefits in a large metropolitan school district with more than 5,000 employees. The state where your school district is located does not have a strong collective negotiations law for public employees. Develop, in writing, a process that you would use to create a voluntary fringe benefits program.

- Visit the payroll office of a school district and discuss how position control is maintained so that someone inside the organization cannot create a fictitious employee who receives a salary.

- Ask a human resources administrator in a school district about the percentage of the personnel budget that goes for workers' compensation claims and discuss if this is a reasonable amount.

CHAPTER FOCUS QUESTIONS

1. Identify the steps in the selection process and explain how they are interrelated.

2. Why is the sequence of steps so important in the selection process?

3. Describe the most common methods of performing a job analysis.

4. How is the job description related to the selection criteria?

5. From an expectancy model perspective, what elements would you include in compensation programs?

6. Describe the variables that affect compensation programs.

7. Define direct compensation and explain what should be taken into consideration in developing such a program.

8. Identify and describe the most common types of mandatory and voluntary fringe benefits.

9. What is the relationship between compensation and higher levels of employee performance?

6

Retaining Generation Y Through Assessment and Professional Growth

CHAPTER OBJECTIVES

The following objectives are the focus of this chapter:

- To provide effective performance evaluation information for Generation Y teachers and administrators
- To understand the expectations of Generation Y teachers that are valid for evaluation purposes
- To provide information regarding traits leading to termination of Generation Y teachers
- To explain professional development opportunities and professional learning community interactions for Generation Y teachers and administrators
- To examine the conditions of learning for Generation Y teachers while providing staff development opportunities

Vignette

Mr. Ramsey has been the principal of a small elementary school for seventeen years. His school provides education for grades K–4 in a rural community, with two to three sections per grade each year, depending on enrollment. While he has teachers at his school from a variety of generations, he realizes that most of the newly hired teachers over the past five years are from Generation Y. During this time, he has noticed that his teachers have not been entirely happy with the professional development opportunities provided by the school. Because Mr. Ramsey has a small staff and operates a school in an area with limited resources, he has tried to provide the best professional development opportunities for the least cost. In doing so, he has not been able to provide choices for professional development opportunities. Instead, he arranges for a workshop or speaker on one topic to come to the school and provides an inservice for all teachers. Some of the topics in the past three years have included multiple intelligences, differentiated instruction, further education on students with physical and mental disabilities, and technology in the classroom. He has the teachers complete a short survey of satisfaction after each inservice session, and he has realized that, over time, these surveys have shown less satisfaction.

As a result of the surveys, Mr. Ramsey decides to approach the situation at a faculty meeting. He asks the teachers to speak freely about what they truly want out of professional development. Three new Generation Y teachers explain that many of the topics were repeating information they already knew because they recently graduated from college. They stated that they would prefer choice in sessions, but if that was not possible, maybe they could work together or with veteran teachers on classroom management—a topic they felt would be much more appropriate for them. Mr. Ramsey realized that the "one size fits all" style that he thought had worked in the past was not the best option now.

CHARACTERISTICS OF GENERATION Y

Generation Y teachers and administrators have reactions to events that require a response. For example, a teacher must require a certain amount of order in his or her classroom. Students who are constantly being disruptive to the instructional-learning process or teachers who are performing at a less than adequate level require a response that will lead to an adjustment in behavior that is acceptable in terms of best practice. Generation Y teachers and principals seem to want to search for ways not only to address the situation but also to alter the situation that requires the reaction. In other words they appear to be proactive in addressing some issues in a policy manner (Half, 2008; Lovely & Buffum, 2007).

In search for the answers to problems and issues, Generation Y teachers and administrators appear to be ready and willing to take a multidisciplinary approach. They are not constrained by just education theory and practice, but willing to find solutions wherever they can be found.

Among Generation Y teachers and administrators, there is a resurgence of interest in personal development. It is a resurgence based on the premise that the core of a person's individual life is constantly in a state of flux but purposefully tending toward becoming rather than regressing. The self-awareness of Generation Y teachers and administrators is seen in their interest in lifestyles that are geared toward becoming a healthier, well-balanced people capable of controlling their life aspirations. Thus, they are keenly aware of the need for staff development not only for their professional lives but also for their personal lives (Half, 2008; Lovely & Buffum, 2007).

In pursuing their professional careers, they value the principal or superintendent who is willing and capable of coaching them in these pursuits. They want a principal or superintendent who they can trust and who is empathetic and genuinely professional. They like continual feedback and are appreciative of the value that performance evaluation can make in their professional careers (Half, 2008; Lovely & Buffum, 2007).

Generation Y teachers and administrators are capable of multitasking, which means that they can do a good job teaching and mentoring students, engaging colleagues on committees and enjoy being members of the learning community. They want to have an impact on their students and colleagues. In all of these endeavors, they are supportive of the merit pay concept because they believe that such a system motivates and rewards those who want to go beyond just the requirements of being a teacher or administrator (Half, 2008; Lovely & Buffum, 2007).

PERFORMANCE ASSESSMENT OF GENERATION Y TEACHERS AND ADMINISTRATORS

All employees should be evaluated. This is important even from an organizational perspective because there is an integral relationship between each employee's performance and the performance of other employees. This begins with the assessment of the superintendent of schools by the board of education and proceeds down through the chain of command, with each administrator evaluating those employees reporting to him. This process applies not only to the professional staff but also to classified employees whose performance should be evaluated by their immediate supervisors (Rebore, 2007).

The last ten years have brought dramatic change in what is understood by quality instruction, which is centered on such variables as teacher qualifications, preparation, performance, and the outcomes of instruction (Cochran-Smith, 2003, p. 95). In this context, it is important for all employees to recognize the positive nature of performance evaluation. Of the six reasons for assessment that follow, only number five could be interpreted as being negative. However, it is a positive reason because students are entitled to the best services possible. Thus, it is not the reasons that make performance assessment a negative experience, but rather, in some school districts, it is the manner in which it is carried out. Procedural due process is an important element because it ensures fairness and the positive effects of performance evaluation (Rebore, 2007).

This is the role that is played by teacher and labor unions; it is also the role of negotiated master contracts. Performance assessment is always considered to be a management prerogative process. However, a master contract negotiated by a teacher or labor union will certainly include a clause on procedural due process that helps to protect employees' rights to fairness. Six fundamental purposes behind assessment for teachers and administrators include:

1. Assessment fosters the self-development of each employee.

2. Assessment helps to identify a variety of tasks that an employee is capable of performing.

3. Assessment helps to identify professional development needs.

4. Assessment helps to improve performance.

5. Assessment helps to determine if an employee should be retained in the school district and how large a salary increase should be given.

6. Assessment helps to determine the placement, transfer, or promotion of an employee.

Parents and taxpayers are demanding increased accountability in employee performance; employees also are demanding accountability in the assessment methods and techniques used in their evaluations. Administrators and supervisors are being asked to defend their evaluations and the procedures they used in making them. Consequently, it is extremely important to develop a consistent benchmark in establishing an assessment process. Of course, employees are evaluated in relation to their job descriptions, which is the criterion against which performance should be measured (Rebore, 2007).

Developing a Performance Assessment Process for Generation Y Teachers and Administrators

The ultimate goal of all school districts is to educate children and adolescents. How this is accomplished depends upon a multitude of subordinate goals and objectives. It is not only organizationally appropriate, but also legally wise for a school board to establish a policy statement on employee appraisal that will serve as one of these supportive goals. Such a policy gives direction to the various administrative divisions of the school district in their development of organizational objectives. A policy statement might read:

The Board of Education recognizes that quality education rests on the quality of instruction, support services, and administration that is provided by teachers, staff members, and administrators. Thus, the Board directs the superintendent of schools to create and implement a process for evaluating all the employees of the school district. It is imperative that the process is fair, impartial, and objective. Further, the process must support the instructional goals of each individual school and the Board of Education.

The organizational culture, as exemplified by the board of education's policies, is critical to understanding the expectations for teachers and administrators (Kelley & Finnigan, 2003, pp. 618–620). The three major divisions in most school districts are human resources, instruction, and support services.

After divisional objectives have been established by the appropriate assistant superintendents, all employees in that division are responsible for developing personal objectives that support the divisional objectives. An assistant superintendent for secondary education might see a need to be present more often in the schools to observe operations firsthand. This would constitute a personal objective to be accomplished over a given period of time. A high school teacher of U.S. history might develop an objective aimed at using more technology in lesson presentations.

The next step in the assessment development process is to decide on formal assessment procedures. These procedures should be in written form and made available to the entire staff. A concern often voiced by employees is that they were not adequately informed about the assessment process. Because assessment procedures are applicable to all school district employees, a common practice is to incorporate them into the board of education's policy manual that is distributed to all employees when they are hired. Other school districts have employee handbooks that outline working conditions and specify the procedures and forms used in the assessment process.

Developing the actual procedures is a task that is best performed by involving employee representatives who both evaluate and will be evaluated. This committee approach produces a sense of involvement and accountability that will help to defend assessment procedures in the face of possible criticism. This is crucial to Generation Y teachers who are used to being included in decision making that affects them.

It is appropriate to divide the employees of the school district into two groups, professional and classified, when organizing the assessment development committees. The work situations of these two groups are significantly different and consequently may necessitate different assessment procedures. It is more defensible to have committee members elected by the employees they represent than to have them appointed. If a school district's employees belong to unions or professional associations, it would be appropriate to have these organizations appoint representatives to serve on the committees.

Of course, the procedures will be tailored to the needs of the individual school district. However, the following questions should be addressed in every set of procedures:

- Who, by position, has the primary responsibility for making evaluations?
- Who is evaluated by these designated positions?
- In what settings will formal evaluations take place?
- On how many occasions will formal evaluations occur?
- In what setting will the results of formal evaluations be communicated to the person evaluated?
- If an employee disagrees with her evaluation, what grievance procedure should be available?
- What effect will assessment have on salary increase?

In analyzing these procedures, it is important to realize that assessment of all employees is a continual and ongoing process. However, it is just as important to have "formal" evaluations when employees can demonstrate their performance capabilities. Formal assessment is applicable to situations that involve interaction between an individual and a defined group. Teachers are subject to this process because of their interaction with students. Principals can be evaluated in this manner on how effectively they handle staff meetings

The final step in the assessment process is analysis of the results that have been obtained through employee evaluations to determine if division objectives are being met. If objectives have not been reached, and if they are still relevant to implementing the objectives and goals of the school board, the divisional objectives should be retargeted. This suggests that the employee objectives apparently did not support the divisional objectives and should be realigned to support them. If both the divisional and employee objectives have been realized, new objectives can be identified that will further the goals of the organization and the development of individual employees.

Constructing Performance Assessment Instruments for Generation Y Teachers and Administrators

As with the development of assessment procedures, assessment instruments should be constructed by the committee process. Many management-consulting firms have developed assessment forms that are easily adapted to the requirements of a given school district. However, the construction of assessment forms is not a difficult task, particularly with the many prototypes available by other school districts.

The basic format of an assessment instrument has certain theoretical overtones. Most authors recognize two basic categories, trait forms and impact forms. In the trait approach, the employees are rated against a predetermined list of indicators in order to ascertain their level of performance. The impact method of assessment contrasts teacher performance with the goals and objectives developed by the teacher with the principal, revealing how such goals and objectives were met (Danielson & McGreal, 2000, pp. 110–114).

Many school districts are using standards that have been developed by several professional associations as guides in constructing performance-based assessment instruments. The Interstate New Teacher Assessment and Support Consortium (INTASC) standards developed under the auspices of the Council of Chief State School Officers (2005) are currently considered to be best practice for licensure requirements in many states. INTASC standards are also compatible with the advanced certification standards of the new National Board for Professional Teaching Standards. These standards can be transformed into performance criteria.

Representatives from the teaching profession, colleges and universities, and representatives from a number of state educational agencies developed the INTASC standards. What follows are the ten core standards that INTASC considers essential for all teachers without regard to the subject or grade level that they teach.

1. The teacher understands the central concepts, tools of inquiry, and structures of the discipline(s) he or she teaches and can create learning experiences that make these aspects of subject matter meaningful for students.

2. The teacher understands how children learn and develop, and can provide learning opportunities that support their intellectual, social, and personal development.

3. The teacher understands how students differ in their approaches to learning and creates instructional opportunities that are adapted to diverse learners.

4. The teacher understands and uses a variety of instructional strategies to encourage students' development of critical thinking, problem solving, and performance skills.

5. The teacher uses an understanding of individual and group motivation and behavior to create a learning environment that encourages positive social interaction, active engagement in learning, and self-motivation.

6. The teacher uses knowledge of effective verbal, nonverbal, and media communication techniques to foster active inquiry, collaboration, and supportive interaction in the classroom.

7. The teacher plans instruction based on knowledge of subject matter, students, the community, and curriculum goals.

8. The teacher understands and uses formal and informal assessment strategies to evaluate and ensure the continuous intellectual, social, and physical development of the learner.

9. The teacher is a reflective practitioner who continually evaluates the effect of his or her choices and actions on others (students, parents, and other professionals in the learning community) and who actively seeks out opportunities to grow professionally.

10. The teacher fosters relationships with school colleagues, parents, and agencies in the larger community to support students' learning and well-being (Council of Chief State School Officers, 2005). The construction of the indicators has been guided not only by the standards but also by the knowledge, dispositions, and performance indicators. Here, for example, are the North Carolina Key Indicators for the first INTASC standard.

The candidate:

- Demonstrates an understanding of the central concepts of his or her discipline
- Uses explanations and representations that link curriculum to prior learning
- Evaluates resources and curriculum materials for appropriateness to the curriculum and instructional delivery
- Engages students in interpreting ideas from a variety of perspectives
- Uses interdisciplinary approaches to teaching and learning
- Uses methods of inquiry that are central to the discipline (North Carolina State Board of Education and Department of Public Instruction, 2005)

Job descriptions play an important role in constructing appraisal instruments and in the developing of objectives. The job requirements of a position are the legal parameters within which assessment must be confined. An employee performs job requirements to an acceptable, unacceptable, or superior level. To require an employee to assume responsibilities that are not within the job description and to evaluate how the employee carries out these responsibilities is poor management. The dismissal of an employee based on gaps in performance responsibilities omitted from the job description may not hold up in court.

Generation Y Teacher and Administrator Inadequate Performance

Adequate performance refers to a condition in an organization created by employees conducting themselves according to the rules and regulations of the organization and in a socially accepted manner. Most individuals are self-disciplined and have little difficulty in following rules and regulations. Also, fellow employees can exert significant pressure on people who violate socially accepted norms. Using inappropriate language is a typical example of conduct offensive to most people.

There are two areas of inadequate performance that call for some action on the part of administrators: excessive absence from work and inappropriate on-the-job behavior. Absenteeism has become a major issue costing literally millions of dollars. One example is that of a newly hired Generation Y teacher who got confused about the days of the week and forgot to show up to school on Monday; she had to be strongly reminded to be more formal about coming to school on time. Many theories have been proposed for this change in work ethic. However, the cause is usually rooted in the person, who must take responsibility for his actions.

"Inappropriate on-the-job behavior" is meant to cover a variety of situations such as carelessness, failure to use safety procedures, fighting, and alcohol and drug abuse. There are a number of variables that affect the seriousness of absenteeism and inappropriate on-the-job behavior. The administration must consider the nature of the problem, the duration of the problem, the frequency of the problem, the employee's work history, and other extenuating factors. However, it is clear to all practicing administrators that a response must be made to correct the problem. The response of the administration to such problems must be corrective rather than punitive, and the action taken must be progressive if it is to withstand the test of "due process."

Developing Termination Procedures for Severe Cases of Inadequate Performance of Generation Y Teachers and Administrators

A universally accepted purpose for evaluating an individual's performance is to make a determination concerning the desirability of retaining that person as an employee of the school district. A decision to dismiss an employee, of course, is extremely difficult to make because of the importance of employment to a person's welfare, and also because of the effects such a decision has on the employee's dependents.

Employment counselors have seen the devastating financial and psychological effects that being fired can have on a person's life. In fact, the trauma usually centers on the individual's self-concept. Feelings of inadequacy, failure, self-contempt, and anger are common to people who have their employment terminated. Although most individuals are able to cope with such a situation, others never fully recover from such an experience. Consequently, it is not only good human resources management, but also a humane responsibility for school district administrators to develop termination procedures that are objective and fair, and that incorporate a due process that gives employees the opportunity to modify or defend their behavior. The Missouri State Statutes Governing Revocation of License, Contract Management, and Termination Procedures present a model that is being used in the following section to explicate the nuances of due process and the grounds for terminating employment. Although the statutes pertain specifically to teachers, the concepts explained are applicable to other categories of employees.

Grounds for Terminating the Employment of Tenured Generation Y Teachers or Administrators

Tenured teachers may have their employment terminated for one or more of the following causes: physical or mental condition unfitting him to instruct or associate with children; immoral conduct; insubordination, inefficiency, or incompetency in the line of duty; willful or persistent violation of, or failure to obey, the state laws pertaining to schools; willful or persistent violation of the published policies and procedures of the school board; excessive or unreasonable absence from work; or conviction of a felony or a crime involving moral turpitude.

The first cause listed must be understood within the context of the Rehabilitation Act of 1973. A disability does not constitute a physical condition that may in any way be construed as unfitting an individual from associating with children or students. Immoral conduct must be judged within the context of local standards, but also must be reasonable and consistent with recent court decisions. A number of significant court cases have been reviewed and form the foundation for the following principles that should be used in judging employee conduct. First, the health of the pupil/teacher relationship is the criterion for judging employee behavior. Insubordination in the line of duty is always a cause for dismissal. Although the interpretation of what constitutes insubordination may appear to be self-evident, insubordination has restricted application. Employees can be insubordinate only if they refuse to comply with a directive of their supervisor that is clearly within their job expertise. Inefficiency is relatively easy to document. It usually refers to the inability of an individual to manage those tasks that are integral to a job responsibility.

Incompetency is perhaps the most difficult cause to document in terminating an employee. It also is directly related to the formal assessment process. If a tenured teacher is performing in an incompetent manner, it means that she is hindering the instructional-learning process. The evaluations made by the principal must clearly indicate that major deficiencies have been identified and that objectives to remedy these deficiencies have not been met.

Claiming willful or persistent violations of state school laws or board of education policies and procedures as a cause for termination presupposes that school district employees have been informed of these. An effective method of notifying employees about these laws, policies, and procedures is through the publication and dissemination of a handbook or manual (in hard copy or available on a Web site) that clearly outlines the employee's responsibilities. Excessive or unreasonable absence from work is a relative circumstance that can be substantiated only through a policy defining what is meant by excessive or unreasonable. Conviction of a felony is obviously a reason to terminate the employment of an individual.

In 1989, Congress passed the Drug-Free Workplace Act, which gives employers the choice of rehabilitating or dismissing staff members working in federal grant programs who are convicted of drug abuse offenses in the workplace. This law and federal administrative regulations require school districts to maintain a drug-free work environment by explicitly prohibiting employees from manufacturing, distributing, dispensing, possessing, or using unlawful drugs in the workplace. In addition, schools must also provide a drug-free awareness program, which must include a description of the dangers of drug abuse, notification of the new requirements and penalties for violations, and information on available employee assistance programs. The characteristics of Generation Y teachers and administrators are the backdrop against which the content of this chapter should be viewed. Generation Y are certainly amenable to coaching and want supervisors who are casual, yet professional. They are willing to take criticism if it will advance their performance and careers.

PROFESSIONAL DEVELOPMENT FOR GENERATION Y TEACHERS AND ADMINISTRATORS

Performance appraisal and professional development are complementary aspects of effective supervision. A professional development program can offer the teacher opportunities to:

- Update skills and knowledge in a subject area
- Keep abreast of societal demands
- Become acquainted with research on the instructional process and on new methods of teaching
- Become acquainted with the advances in instructional materials and equipment

A second source of information is the community survey, which is administered to parents, usually through a school-based organization such as the Parent-Teacher Association. This survey may reveal parental concerns about a wide range of issues such as grading, student groupings, discipline, and drug use by students (Rebore, 2007).

Third, certification requirements vary from state to state and occasionally change. The director of professional development needs to keep all teachers and other certificated employees informed about requirements and should plan appropriate credit courses on both an off-campus and on-campus basis. The human resources master plan also will provide the director with information about the future needs of the district in relation to certain categories of certificated employees (Rebore, 2007).

The final source of information is curricular research. Professional development programs can be planned to correlate with future curriculum changes. Research points to future skills and competencies that can be acquired and gradually introduced to ensure an even transition. The historic report, *A Nation at Risk* (Milton & Harvey, 1983), published by the National Commission on Excellence in Education, was the impetus for many states to pass legislation centered on improving the quality of education. Much of this legislation calls for the establishment of professional development committees composed of teachers and other staff members who are responsible for assisting the administration in identifying the professional development needs of teachers. Along with the administration, these committees are also involved in the creation of professional development delivery systems.

Change is a constant occurrence in contemporary society. Instant-communication channels produced by technological advances present students and educators with changes in politics, economics, science, and social status from every corner of the world. The mandate of public schools, of course, is to educate the children, adolescents, and young adults of our country in order to help them meet the challenges that tomorrow will bring as a result of these changes. As an organization, a school district needs well-qualified administrators, teachers, and support personnel to fulfill this mandate. As the positions and job requirements within a school district become more complex, the importance of professional development programs increases.

Professional development practices have undergone considerable change over the last two decades. Two trends that have contributed to this metamorphosis are results-driven education, the systems approach to school and school district organization, and constructivism. As a practice, results-driven professional development is concerned with changing the behavior and attitudes of teachers, administrators, and staff members rather than being concerned with the number of participants in such programs. The constructivist approach emphasizes the phenomenon by which learners build knowledge structures in their minds rather than receiving the knowledge from instruction. Thus, professional development should include action research and mentoring programs in contrast to the more traditional milieu through which programs are delivered (Sparks, 1994, p. 42).

It is literally impossible today for any individual to take on a job or enter a profession and remain in it for forty or so years with his skills basically unchanged. Since Generation Y embraces feedback and change, professional development is not only desirable but also an activity to which each school system must commit human and fiscal resources if it is to maintain a skilled and knowledgeable staff. However, professional development must be productive for the teachers—it should not be a repeat of something Generation Y teachers just had in their teacher training. Having choice for teachers would improve the outcomes of successful professional development programs.

Professional Learning Communities as the Foundation for Professional Development for Generation Y Teachers and Administrators

As a dimension of the human resources function, professional development can be organized according to various structures. Currently, the most effective structure is probably the professional learning community. Such a structure has four major focuses: (1) learning rather than teaching, (2) collaboration, (3) viewing all members of the community as learners, and (4) self-accountability.

The first focus is a departure from the traditional approach to educating students, which centers on the responsibility of schools and school districts to ensure effective teaching. When the focus is placed on learning, teachers, administrators, and staff members tend to see their responsibilities in a different light. They begin to analyze the culture of the school and school district in order to ascertain whether it supports student learning. Further, teachers, administrators, and staff members begin to understand that effective school and school district cultures are founded on a commitment to learning that must be articulated to all stakeholders, which includes students and parents. It is important to keep in mind that the term "staff members" refers to guidance counselors, media specialists, special education teachers, assistant superintendents for instruction, human resources administrators, and all other professional and support members of the school and school district community.

Of course, this focus on learning that can be investigated through cultural analyses and commitment leads to the second focus, which is collaboration. Teachers, administrators, and staff members must collaboratively discourse and investigate what students need to learn, how to assess what students have learned, and how to help students who are having difficulty learning. Generation Y teachers appreciate this constant communication and collaboration. In addition, they like choice and professional development that is differentiated to meet their specific needs. Collaboration also means that teachers, administrators, and staff members will recognize that every aspect of the learning process is subject to team efforts. For example, if certain students are having difficulty learning, assisting these students is not the responsibility of only their classroom teachers. All members of the community who have related expertise will formulate a timely and required intervention plan to help each student. The usual format for collaboration is teaming, whereby a number of different teams of teachers, administrators, and staff members come together based on the expertise of the individual members in order to address common professional issues. Once formed, a given team may meet on a continual basis or only when necessary.

The third focus of professional learning communities empowers all members of the school and school district communities, not just students, to become learners. Of course, the most fundamental reality of this focus is that everything in life continually changes. Thus, it is impossible for anyone to know all that he or she needs to know all of the time in order to effectively carry out his or her responsibilities. Consequently, parents, teachers, administrators, and staff members are constantly in need of acquiring new information, knowledge, skills, and attitudes. It is impossible to remain static in the dynamic environments of schools and school districts. This, of course, is the domain of professional development.

The final focus centers on self-accountability. The notion of professional learning communities rests on the ability of all members to self-actualize in a manner that contributes to the mission of their respective schools and school districts (DuFour, 2004, pp. 6–11).

Adult Learning in Relation to Generation Y Teachers and Administrators

Adult learning usually consists of two processes, training and education. Training is the process of learning a sequence of programmed behaviors. Administrative assistants, custodians, cooks, and maintenance personnel thus can be trained because their job-related activities are capable of being broken down and analyzed in order to determine the best way to perform certain tasks. In this connotation, training is the application of knowledge that provides employees with a set of procedures that will guide their work-related behaviors (Decenzo & Robbins, 2002).

The emphasis in the training component of a professional development program is on the acquisition of motor skills and on producing simple conditioning methods that will improve employees' abilities to perform their jobs. Education is the process of helping an individual understand and interpret knowledge. Education emphasizes acquiring sound reasoning processes rather than learning a body of serial facts. Education helps an employee develop a rational approach toward analyzing the relationship between variables and consequently understanding phenomena (Decenzo & Robbins, 2002).

Teachers and administrators have job responsibilities that, in most respects, require education rather than training. Teachers and administrators usually do not perform programmed work. For example, an administrator can be trained in management techniques and procedures; however, an administrator cannot be trained to manage (Decenzo & Robbins, 2002).

In discussing the distinction between training and education, care must be taken not to assume that all job-related activities of a particular position are either trainable or educable. Teachers and administrators perform some activities that can be enhanced by training because these activities are capable of being programmed. Both teachers and administrators need good listening skills and interviewing skills; in today's automated society, they also need skills in using the computer. However, understanding the instructional-learning process and being able to create a learning environment conducive to teaching goes beyond the scope of training and requires education (Decenzo & Robbins, 2002).

A professional development program centers around creating instructional-learning situations. Consequently, those charged with organizing such a program must have a profound understanding of the psychology and conditions required for effective learning. Numerous theories have been proposed about how learning occurs. This chapter will not elucidate all the principles described by these theories, but rather will present those aspects of learning common to the major theories (Decenzo & Robbins, 2002).

Learning is a change in human capability that can be retained and that is not simply ascribable to the process of growth. The manifestation of change, as described in this definition, is the behavior of the learner. The extent to which learning has occurred is measured by comparing those behaviors that were present before the individual was placed in the instructional-learning situation against those behaviors that can be demonstrated after the experience. The desired change is usually an increased skill or capability of more than momentary significance (Decenzo & Robbins, 2002).

Changes in behavior are brought about by four basic learning conditions: stimulus, response, reinforcement, and motivation. A stimulus is someone or something that initiates an action. An instructor will stimulate a learner by asking a question. The learner answering the question makes a response. If the instructor responds to the learner with, "That is a correct and appropriate answer," the learner is receiving reinforcement. Finally, if the learner perceives completion of the course of instruction as a means of obtaining a job, a promotion, a raise in salary, or some other desired goal, the learner is said to have motivation. Although this explanation of the four basic components of learning is rather simplistic, it does present the necessary conditions for learning to take place (Decenzo & Robbins, 2002).

Considerations that impinge on these conditions of learning should be mentioned here for the sake of completeness, but they will not be elaborated on to any great extent. First, a certain amount of planning must precede the instructional learning situation to determine the most appropriate learning structure for the subject matter that will be taught. In learning, every new capability builds on a foundation established by previously learned capabilities. Planning specifies and orders these prerequisite capabilities so that that a learning objective can be reached. For example, a professional development workshop designed to help teachers construct metric system materials for classroom use should be preceded by a seminar explaining the metric system to teachers who are not proficient with the system (Decenzo & Robbins, 2002).

Second, the environment of learning must be effectively managed. Those responsible for planning should ask themselves what is the most appropriate time and setting to carry out instruction. A comfortable and stimulating environment certainly enhances learning, and especially for adult learners, the instruction should take place at a time of day when they are not fatigued. This suggests that certain professional development seminars, workshops, or courses for teachers should be scheduled on days when school is not in session. This also implies that an effective professional development program should provide employees with released time from their regular duties so they can attend during the working day (Decenzo & Robbins, 2002).

Third, instruction must have some practical application for the adult learner. Adults generally can learn more material in less time than children, but they must see that the material can help them in their work. For example, a school bus driver who attends a workshop on managing student behavior must be shown techniques that can actually be used with disruptive students (Decenzo & Robbins, 2002).

Fourth, learning rarely takes place at a constant rate; rather, it fluctuates according to the difficulty of the subject matter or skill to be learned and the ability of the learner. Developing keyboarding skills is a good example. During the first three months of instruction, the learner becomes familiar with the keyboard and basic techniques. During the next three months, the individual develops speed, and learning accelerates. After six months of instruction, learning normally slows down because the individual has progressed to the point of technique refinement (Decenzo & Robbins, 2002).

Creating a Professional Development Program for Generation Y Teachers and Administrators

Experience has taught human resources administrators the folly of approaching professional development merely from the "Let's have a workshop" model. This traditional concept of what was, and is still, referred to in some school districts as "inservice training" or "staff training" has severe limitations, not only in scope but also in effectiveness. Rather, the concept of "professional development" addresses the real needs of educational organizations. The evolution of this approach is mirrored in all of our societal institutions. In the past, changes were thrust upon the schools without giving teachers and administrators an opportunity to prepare for such changes.

During the last decade, there has been a myriad of research on professional development. Most of this research has centered on identifying those variables that produce effective professional development programs. As a consequence of this research, many models have been created. Some of the most often proposed in professional development literature are Program for Effective Teaching (PET), Readiness, Planning, Training, Implementation, Maintenance (RPTIM), Concern-Based Adoption Model (CBAM), and Professional Development for School Improvement (PDSI). A common thread connecting all these models is the goal of producing effective instruction through clinical supervision. As principals evaluate and supervise teachers in order to improve instruction, professional development programs become a vehicle through which teachers can enhance skills and remedy deficiencies. This is crucial for Generation Y teachers as they continue to adapt to an interactive and collaborative working environment.

Some employees perceive professional development activities as ineffective because they receive little support for implementing newly acquired skills and ideas. Other conditions that affect the success of a professional development program include lack of appropriate program organization and lack of supervision during implementation. Clearly, these conditions are symptomatic of a more fundamental problem, the lack of commitment. In any organization, this commitment must emanate from the highest level of responsibility down through the various levels of administration to the employees. In order to be effective, the board of education must support the program; the administration must organize and supervise the program; and the employees must participate in program planning.

In delineating the tasks to be performed by the various components of a school district, the board of education must set the stage by creating a positive climate for the program and by providing the necessary fiscal funding and appropriate policies for implementation. The central-office administration, through the director of professional development, is responsible for creating a master plan and for overall management and supervision of the program. Building principals and supervisors are responsible for identifying the knowledge, skills, and abilities that are needed to carry out the goals and objectives of the school district. Teachers and staff members are responsible for participating not only in program planning but also in the programs. Consequently, the success of a professional development program depends on the commitment of each individual within each level of the school district.

SCHOOL DISTRICT GOALS AND OBJECTIVES IN RELATION TO GENERATION Y TEACHERS AND ADMINISTRATORS

Educational goals and objectives, taken in the broadest sense, are similar across the country. Schools are concerned about educating children in the basic skills and developing in our children those cultural values that will perpetuate our American heritage. The genesis of a professional development program, therefore, originates from educational goals and objectives. When these goals and objectives are formulated into written policies of the board of education, a professional development program has the guidance necessary for integrating the individual goals of employees with those of the school district.

The primary purpose of a professional development program is to increase the knowledge and skills of employees and thereby increase the potential of the school district to attain its goals and objectives. The process of assessing employee needs is essentially the process of determining the discrepancy between the existing and the needed competencies of the teaching staff. This analysis also must consider projected human resources needs. Thus, a professional development program must be concerned not only with the abilities of individuals currently occupying positions, but also with the abilities individuals need to qualify for promotion to positions of more responsibility. The data obtained from the human resources inventories used in the human resources planning process, along with the data obtained from needs assessment techniques provide the framework within which program goals and objectives can be established.

Professional development goals and objectives continually change to meet the needs of individual staff members and the school district. A predominantly European American suburban school district that begins to get an influx of African American families might consider creating a program for the administrative, teaching, and support staffs on the impact that the mingling of these two distinctive American cultures will have on the functioning of the school district. Another example might be that the purchase of new computer equipment will create a need to instruct the office staff on its most effective use.

These examples of changes that affect the operations of a school district should be more broadly formulated into goals and objectives. For example, a professional development goal involving integration might be stated as follows: "to prepare the administration, teachers, and staff to effectively address the integration of African American students into the school community." Objectives specifying this goal could be formulated as follows:

- To develop a sense of appreciation for cultural differences on the part of teachers, administrators, and staff members
- To develop strategies that will help students acquire an understanding of different cultures

Such a goal, with accompanying objectives, provides direction to the next phase in creating a professional development program. Designing a program involves more than simply finding a university professor who is interested in giving a workshop on a particular topic. Broadly conceived, program design is a process of matching needs with available resources through an effective delivery method. Therefore, it is unproductive to assign or endorse an activity without considering how this activity helps to meet goals and objectives. A variety of resource people will also enhance a professional development program. Among the most available and knowledgeable persons are teachers, senior staff members, college and university professors, professional consultants, journal authors, teacher organization representatives, and administrators. Group-oriented design has proven to be an effective method for delivering professional development programs. With collaboration and group work an integral part of Generation Y teachers, this type of program is ideal. Individualized programs are another alternative to the traditional program design model. Such programs allow the individual maximum creativity in matching personal interests and needs to the goals and objectives of the school district. Teachers who engage in personalized activities usually improve their teaching skills. These activities include the following:

- Serving on curriculum research and improvement committees
- Professional publications and activities such as writing journal articles and initiating action research
- Attending professional conferences
- Sponsoring extramural activities for students and informational activities for parents

A critical aspect in all professional development programs is the implementation and delivery phase. The very best of intentions and planning may fail unless attention is paid to providing employees with appropriate incentives to participate, making satisfactory time arrangements, and handling ordinary organizational problems. Although direct payment in the form of salary increments is a proven incentive, indirect financial aid is more influential in promoting participation in professional development programs.

Time is a valuable commodity to all employees and, thus, it is a key factor in organizing and encouraging employee participation in development programs. There is a growing trend to incorporate professional development programs as part of the working day or, at least, as an extension of the day. Some school districts set aside a number of afternoons each month for development programs; others bring courses and lectures directly to the schools. Whatever the arrangement for delivering a professional development program, experience indicates that the least effective time is after a full day of teaching or work. No teacher, administrator, or employee will be able to assimilate new ideas when fatigued.

A final consideration in administering a professional development program is providing the administrative mechanism to handle the ordinary problems that occur in all human interaction. Some specific problems that tend to hinder employee participation include not understanding the purpose or expected transference of the program content to practice in the classroom.

Effective assessment is the final phase in a professional development program. Some school districts see this as a rather complicated task involving multiple applications of statistics; others neglect it entirely. For most programs, a perception-based approach is both appropriate and effective. Participants are asked to rate the instructor or individual conducting the program, the content of the program, how the program was organized, and the time and place of the program presentation.

SUMMARY

The reasons that justify the establishment and implementation of an assessment process for all school district employees include the following: to foster self-development, to identify a variety of tasks, which an employee is capable of performing, to identify professional development needs, to improve employee performance, to determine if an employee should be retained and what her salary increase should be, and to help in the proper placement or promotion of an employee. A significant aspect of an appraisal process is measuring employees' performance against their job responsibilities as outlined in respective job descriptions.

As a dimension of the human resources function, professional development can be organized according to various structures. Currently, the most effective structure is probably the professional learning community. Such a structure has four major focuses: learning rather than teaching, collaboration, viewing all members of the community as learners, and self-accountability.

In all learning environments, four basic components must be present to ensure success: stimulus, response, reinforcement, and motivation. Creating a professional development program consists of six separate but sequential processes: (1) establishing school district goals and objectives, which become the foundation of the program; (2) assessing the needs of the school district employees to determine if there is a discrepancy between the competencies of the staff and the requirements of the organization; (3) establishing professional development goals and objectives; (4) designing a program that will meet the professional development requirements; (5) implementing the designed plan in such a way that effective learning may occur; and (6) evaluating the program to ascertain if it is meeting its objectives, which in turn will affect future program designs.

CASE STUDY

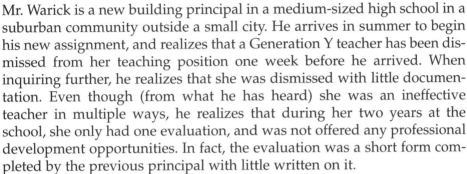

Mr. Warick is a new building principal in a medium-sized high school in a suburban community outside a small city. He arrives in summer to begin his new assignment, and realizes that a Generation Y teacher has been dismissed from her teaching position one week before he arrived. When inquiring further, he realizes that she was dismissed with little documentation. Even though (from what he has heard) she was an ineffective teacher in multiple ways, he realizes that during her two years at the school, she only had one evaluation, and was not offered any professional development opportunities. In fact, the evaluation was a short form completed by the previous principal with little written on it.

After hearing this information, Mr. Warick inquires about other teacher evaluations in the past and realizes that the previous principal was not consistent in doing evaluations, and the evaluation form was not consistent among teachers. In fact, the two main evaluation forms he found were so old that they were type-written and there exists no electronic version. When investigating past professional development opportunities, it appears they were poorly scheduled and not well attended. He is worried that teacher professionalism and morale is low. He knew that his new position would be challenging, but he initially only thought of the challenge in dealing with poorly prepared students and interactions with parents and the community—he had no idea he would face many challenges with teacher preparation, background, or evaluations. Wanting to create a strong school with new and veteran teachers, while supporting and encouraging professional growth, he worries about how and where to start.

Analyze the scenario described above by answering the following questions:

- What steps regarding teacher evaluation should Mr. Warick make to ensure fair and consistent evaluations between all teachers that can be useful for professional growth?
- What issues should Mr. Warick address with Generation Y teachers who may be worried about their own jobs after the termination of their colleague over the summer?
- What types of professional development should Mr. Warick consider for the teachers in his building who have not had many positive experiences with professional development recently?
- What types of learning styles and interactions for professional development should Mr. Warick be aware of when integrating the Baby Boomer, Generation X, and Generation Y teachers?

- What types of professional development opportunities should Mr. Warick offer and promote for these teachers who have had minimal opportunities in the past?
- How can Mr. Warick begin to create a positive learning community?

EXERCISES

1. You are the assistant superintendent for human resources in a school district with approximately 500 employees. Develop a due process procedure for the employee termination that you believe is both humane and also meets the responsibility of the board of education. Write a comparison of your procedure with the statutes that govern the termination process in the state where you live.

2. In writing, compare and contrast these same state statutes and your procedure with the principles for teacher termination in this chapter.

3. Construct what you think is an ideal administrator assessment form.

4. Interview a human resources administrator in person or on the telephone about how the performance assessment and termination processes are interrelated and further discuss the practical implications of both processes.

5. You are the director of professional development for a school district with 250 teachers and 9 administrators. The state legislature has just mandated that 1 percent of a school district's state aid must be used for teacher professional development. Thus, you have approximately $150,000 to spend on professional development. Describe, in writing, the aspects of a professional development program that you would develop with the money. Begin by stating the program goals and objectives.

6. Obtain the policies of a school district on professional development. Write a comparison of the policies with the principles set forth in this chapter.

7. Obtain needs assessment surveys that are being used in a school district to create professional development programs for administrators, teachers, and classified employees. Using the principles in this chapter, write an analysis of the surveys.

8. Interview a director of professional development in person or on the telephone concerning the strategies that can be used to create and deliver effective professional development programs for Generation Y teachers.

CHAPTER FOCUS QUESTIONS

1. What is the rationale for the performance assessment of employees?

2. How does performance assessment benefit both the employee and the school district?

3. Explain how performance assessment can be an integral component of effective supervision.

4. What type of assessment report forms do you think are the most effective?

5. Explain the relationship between the performance goals and objectives of the school district and of individual employees.

6. Explain how professional development is related to the performance assessment of employees.

7. Discuss the benefits of effective professional development programs for Generation Y teachers.

8. What are some strategies that can be used to motivate Generation Y employees to participate in professional development programs?

9. How might the principles of adult learning influence the creation of professional development programs?

10. What types of professional development programs are best suited for Generation Y employees in classified positions?

11. Identify and describe professional development programs that are most beneficial for building administrators.

Resource

Definitions of Technological Items and Terms

blog: A "web log" used as an online journal to post thoughts, commentary, videos, and graphics.

Bluetooth: A device that connects to electronics to allow for short-range wireless communication.

broadband internet service: High-speed internet access that performs faster than dial-up service.

browser: An application used to search and display Web sites based on specified keywords.

CD-ROM: A compact disc that uses read-only memory to store large amounts of data that cannot be erased and filled with new information.

CD-RW: A compact disc that uses rewritable memory to store large amounts of data that can be written and changed multiple times.

chat room: Online conferencing through the sending of text messages between individuals in real-time.

dial-up service: Internet access that uses a modem connected to a telephone line.

document camera and digital overhead: A document scanning device that uses a video camera to display images in real time.

DVR: Digital video recorder, used to record and store video in a digital format.

e-mail: Electronic mail that uses text communication sent via computers connected by an external network.

emoticon: Adjacent symbols created by keystrokes that portray emotions in a visual, written format.

ERIC: Educational Resources Information Center, a popular online digital library of educational literature (e.g., journal articles, books, research papers).

Ethernet: The framework for connecting devices to a local-area network that supports data transfer.

Facebook and MySpace: Social networking Web sites that allow sharing of personal information, photos, and videos.

firewall: An internal barrier on a computer to enforce security policies and protect damaging software from gaining access to the computer through a sharing network or the Internet.

forum: An internet discussion site that allows participants to view and contribute posts on a specified topic.

homepage: The main page of a Web site that initially opens when the Web address is loaded.

hotspot: Any location where it is possible to connect to wireless internet services.

IM: Instant messaging, online communication in real time that uses text messages sent via computers connected by an external network or the Internet.

iPod: A portable audio and video player created by Apple®.

ISTE®: The International Society for Technology in Education, the largest teacher-based, nonprofit organization dedicated to advancing the field of educational technology in the classroom.

LAN: Local-area network, a network of communicating computers within a small, locally connected area.

modem: The communication device that allows a computer to connect to the Internet and transmit information over a telephone line or cable.

MP3: A compressed, digital audio file.

network: A group of connected computers that can share resources, exchange files, and allow electronic communication.

PDF file: Portable document format, developed by Adobe that preserves the elements of a printed document in the form of an electronic image so people can view, print, or electronically send information.

podcast: Audio and video files distributed via the Internet as a form of blogging that can be viewed and/or listened to through a portable media player (e.g., iPod) or computer.

ProQuest: An online digital library that provides access to databases of articles organized by various disciplines.

QWERTY: The description for the arrangement of keys on a standard keyboard.

router: The hardware that assigns addresses to devices within a local-area network and controls the transfer of data between those devices.

scanner: A device that optically scans documents of printed text and graphics to convert them into a digital image to be viewed and stored on a computer.

search engine: An online site that searches for documents based on specified keywords and displays the relevant documents.

server: The computer that is designated to serve as the controller of a local-area network.

Skype: Software that allows calls to be made via the Internet.

SIM card: A small, portable memory chip placed inside a cellular phone to allow easy transfer of information to a new phone.

SMART board: An interactive, touch-sensitive whiteboard that works in conjunction with a computer and digital projector to manipulate text and images, write notes in digital ink, save created work, showcase student presentations, and write notes over video clips (Smart Technologies, Inc., 2006).

spam: A form of unsolicited commercial e-mail sent in bulk to a large number of people.

telecommute: To work at a location outside of one's place of employment by using devices such as a computer, telephone, and fax to communicate job assignments.

texting: Sending text messages via cellular phones.

thumb drive, jump drive, or flash drive: A small, portable memory-storage device that can be used to serve as short-term backup of data or transfer files from one computer to another by fitting into the USB port of a computer.

USB: Universal Serial Bus, serves as a standard connection portal for a computer.

videoconference: A discussion in real time between groups of people in different locations via electronic communication devices that display participants on video screens.

webcam: A small video camera attached to a computer that transmits images via the Internet. It is often used for videoconferencing.

webcast: Live or prerecorded audio and/or video files broadcasted via the Internet.

WebQuest: A time-efficient, inquiry-oriented activity in which most or all of the information that learners interact with comes from online resources. It is used in order for learners to transform what is being learned into meaningful understandings and real-world projects (Lamb, 2004).

wi-fi: Wireless access to the Internet through radio waves.

wiki: A Web page or compilation of Web pages designed to enable individuals to contribute to its collection of content. A well-known wiki in the form of a collaborative online encyclopedia is Wikipedia.

wireless network: A service that allows a computer to access the Internet without being directly connected into a cable.

workstations: The computers that are connected to the server of a designated local-area network.

YouTube: An online database that allows users to upload and view video clips.

References

Au, K. H., & Blake, K. M. (2003). Cultural identity and learning to teach in a diverse community: Findings from a collective case study. *Journal of Teacher Education, 54* (3), 192–205.

Babcock, P. (2005). Find what workers want. *HR Magazine, 50* (4), 50–57.

Busher, H. (2005). The project of the other: Developing inclusive learning communities in school. *Oxford Review of Education, 31* (4), 461–462.

Cochran-Smith, M. (2003). Teaching quality matters. *Journal of Teacher Education: The Journal of Policy, Practice, and Research in Teacher Education, 54* (2), 95.

Coomes, M. D., & DeBard, R. (Eds.). (2004). *New directions for student services*. San Francisco: Jossey-Bass.

Council of Chief State School Officers. (2005). *Interstate New Teacher Assessment and Support Consortium (INTASC)*. Retrieved May 18, 2009, from http://www .ccsso.org/Projects/interstate_new_teacher_assessment_and_support_ consortium/780.cfm.

Cunningham, W. C., & Cordeiro, P. A. (2000). *Educational administration: A problem-based approach*. Boston: Allyn & Bacon.

Danielson, C., & McGreal, T. L. (2000). *Teacher evaluation: To enhance professional practice*. Princeton, NJ: Educational Testing Service.

DeBard, R. (2004). Millennials coming to college. *New Directions for Student Services, 106*, 40.

Decenzo, D. A., & Robbins, S. P. (2002). *Human resources management* (7th ed.). New York: Wiley & Sons.

DuFour, R. (2004). What is professional learning community? *Educational Leadership, 61* (8), 6–11.

Dvinicki, M. (2004). *Learning and motivation in the postsecondary classroom*. Bolton: Anker Publishing.

Elias, M., Hunter, L., & Kress, J. (2001). Emotional intelligence and education. In J. Ciarrochi, J. P. Forgas, & J. D. Mayer (Eds.), *Emotional intelligence in everyday life: An introduction* (pp. 139–140). New York: Psychology Press.

Fielder, D. J. (1993). Wanted, minority teachers. *The Executive Educator, 15* (5), 33–34.

Fink, L. D. (2003). *Creating significant learning experiences*. San Francisco: Jossey-Bass.

Fogarty, R., & Stoehr, J. (2008). *Integrating curricula with multiple intelligences*. Thousand Oaks, CA: Corwin.

Futernick, K. (2007). A possible dream: Retaining California teachers so all students learn. *California State University Report*, 1–2.

Gallagher, D., Bagin, D., & Morre, M. (2005). *The school and community relations.* Boston: Allyn & Bacon.

Garvey, C. (2001). Outsourcing background checks. *HR Magazine, 46* (3), 95–104.

Goleman, D. (1995). *Emotional intelligence.* New York: Bantam Books.

Half, R. (2008). Attracting and retaining millennial workers. *Information Executive, 11* (7), 2–14.

Howe, N., & Strauss, W. (2000). *Millennials rising: The next great generation.* New York: Vintage Books.

Howe, N., & Strauss, W. (2007). *Millennials go to college.* LifeCourse Associates: Great Falls, VA.

The Internet Center for Management and Business Administration. (2007). *Herzberg's motivation-hygiene theory (two factor theory).* Retrieved May 18, 2009, from http://www.netmba.com/mgmt/ob/motivation/herzberg/

Kelley, C. J., & Finnigan, K. (2003). The effects of organizational context on teacher expectancy. *Educational Administration Quarterly, 39* (5), 618–620.

Kiviat, B. (2009). Jobs are the new assets. *Time Magazine Annual Special Issue, 173* (11), 46–47.

Kopkowski, C. (2007). *Why they leave.* NEA Today 2008 Archives. Retrieved May 18, 2009, from http://www.nea.org/home/12630.htm

Lamb, A. (2004). Key words in instruction. WebQuests. *School Library Media Activities Monthly, 2* (2), 38–40.

Levine, A., & Cureton, J. (1998). What we know about today's college students. *About Campus, 3* (1), 4–9.

Lovely, S., & Buffum, A. J. (2007). *Generations at school: Building an age-friendly learning community.* Thousand Oaks, CA: Corwin.

Lubman, S. (1993, September 7). Efforts to hire minority educators aim to narrow student-teacher ethnic gap. *Wall Street Journal,* pp. B1, B9.

Marvel, J., Lyter, D. M., Peltola, P., Strizek, G. A., & Morton, B. A. (2006). *Teacher Attrition and Mobility: Results from the 2004–05 Teacher Follow-up Survey* (NCES 2007-307). U.S. Department of Education, National Center for Education Statistics. Washington, DC: U.S. Government Printing Office.

Mason, R., & Randell, S. (1995). Democracy, subsidiarity and community-based adult education. *Convergence, 28* (1), 24.

Mayer, J. (2001). A field guide to emotional intelligence. In J. Ciarrochi, J. P. Forgas, & J. D. Mayer (Eds.), *Emotional intelligence in everyday life: An introduction* (p. 24). New York: Psychology Press.

Milton, G., & Harvey, J. (1983). A nation at risk: The report of the National Commission on Excellence in Education. *Phi Delta Kappan, 65* (1), 14–18.

North Carolina State Board of Education and Department of Public Instruction. (2005). *The INTASC Standards.* Retrieved May 18, 2009, from www.dpi.state.nc.us/pbl/pblintasc.htm.

Office of Diversity, Honolulu Community College. (n.d.). *Tips to improve interaction among the generations.* Retrieved May 18, 2009, from http://honolulu.hawaii.edu/intranet/committees/FacDevCom/guidebk/teachtip/intergencomm.htm.

Pletka, B. (2007), *The Net generation.* Santa Monica, CA: Santa Monica Press.

Provenzo, E., & Gotthoffer, D. (2000). *Quick guide to the Internet for education.* Boston: Allyn & Bacon.

Rebore, R. W. (2003). *A human relations approach to the practice of educational leadership.* Boston: Allyn & Bacon.

Rebore, R. W. (2007). *Human resources administration in education: A management approach* (8th ed.). Boston: Allyn & Bacon.

Rebore, R. W., & Walmsley, A. L. (2007). *An evidence-based approach to the practice of educational leadership.* Boston: Allyn & Bacon.

Smart Technologies, Inc. (2006). *Interactive whiteboards and learning: Improving student learning outcomes and streamlining lesson planning.* Retrieved May 18, 2009, from http://www2.smarttech.com/NR/rdonlyres/2C729F6E-0A8D-42B8-9B32-F90BE0A746D8/0/Int_Whiteboard_Research_Whitepaper_Update.pdf

Sparks, D. (1994). A paradigm shift in professional development. *Education Week, 16,* 42.

Stites, J. (2005). Equal pay for the sexes. *HR Magazine, 50* (5), 65–69.

Swann, P. A. (2006). Got Web? Investing in a district Website. *School Administrator, 63* (5), 24–27, 29.

Tapscott, D. (1998). *Growing up digital: The rise of the Net Generation.* New York: McGraw Hill.

Teachers: Recruit, train, and retain the best and the brightest. (2001). White House Education Issues. Retreived November 1, 2008, from http://www.whitehouse.gov/issues/education/

Ubben, G., Hughes, L., & Norris, C. (2001). *The principal: Creative leadership for effective schools.* Boston: Allyn & Bacon.

Walmsley, A., & McManemy, J. (2008). College student character dysfunction. *Academe, 94* (1). Retrieved May 18, 2009, from www.aaup.org/AAUP/pubsres/academe/2008/JF/Feat/walm.htm

Webb, L. D., & Norton, M. S. (2009). *Human resources administration: Personnel issues and needs in education* (5th ed.). Upper Saddle River, NJ: Merrill/Prentice Hall.

Wong, H. K., & Wong, R. T. (n.d.). Teachers: The next generation. *ASCD Express.* Retrieved on May 18, 2009, from http://www.newteacher.com/pdf/ascd_express_wong_teachers.pdf

Young, I. P. (2008). *The human resource function in educational administration* (9th ed.). Upper Saddle River, NJ: Merrill/Prentice Hall.

Young, I. P., & Castetter, W. B. (2003). *The human resources function in educational administration* (8th ed.). Upper Saddle River, NJ: Merrill/Prentice Hall.

Suggested Reading

CHAPTER 1: CHARACTERISTICS OF THE NEW GENERATION OF TEACHERS

Barrett, L. F., & Gross, J. J. (2001). Emotional intelligence: A process model of emotion representation and regulation. In T. J. Mayne & G. A. Bonanno (Eds.), *Emotions: Current issues and future directions* (pp. 286–310). New York: Guildford Press.

Gardner, H. (1999). Are there additional intelligences? In *Intelligence reframed* (pp. 47–66). New York: Basic Books.

Gardner, H. (1999). The theory of multiple intelligences: A personal perspective. In *Intelligence reframed* (pp. 27–46). New York: Basic Books.

Lovely, S., Austin, G. B., & Roland S. B. (2007). Here come the Millennials, ready or not! In *Generations at school: Building an age-friendly learning community* (pp. 71–88). New York: Corwin.

Lyons, S. T., Suxbury, L., & Higgins, C. (2007). An empirical assessment of generational differences in basic human values. *Psychological Reports, 101,* 339–352.

NAS Recruitment. (2006). *Generation Y: The Millennials: Ready or not, here they come.* White paper. Retrieved May 19, 2009, from www.nasrecruitment.com/TalentTips/NASinsights/GenerationY.pdf

CHAPTER 2: MARKETING AND RECRUITING GENERATION Y TEACHERS, STAFF MEMBERS, AND ADMINISTRATORS

Au, K. H., & Blake, K. M. (2003). Cultural identity and learning to teach in a diverse community: Findings from a collective case study. *Journal of Teacher Education, 54* (3), 192–205.

Cunningham, W. G., & Cordeiro, P. A. (2006). *Educational leadership: A problem-based approach* (3rd ed.). Upper Saddle River, NJ: Pearson.

Heneman, H. G., & Judge, T. A. (2006). *Staffing organizations* (6th ed.). Middleton, WI: McGraw Hill.

Ingersoll, R. M. (2002) The teacher shortage: A case of wrong diagnosis. *Bulletin,* *86* (631), 16–30.

Kruse, S. D., & Louis, K. S. (2008). *Building strong school cultures: A guide to leading change.* Thousand Oaks, CA: Corwin.

Liu, E., Johnson, S. M., & Peske, H. G. (2004). New teachers and the Massachusetts signing bonus: The limits of inducements. *Educational Evaluation and Policy Analysis, 26* (3), 217–236.

Winter, P. A., & Morgenthal, J. R. (2002). Principal marketing and recruitment in a reform environment: Effects of school achievement and school level on applicant attraction to the job. *Educational Administration Quarterly, 38* (3), 319–340.

Workman, T. A. (2008). Virtual worlds' real impact: How digital culture shapes students' minds. *The Chronicle Review: A Weekly Review of Ideas, 55* (4), B12–14.

CHAPTER 3: CULTURE OF THE SCHOOL AS GENERATIONS MERGE

Lovely, S., Austin, G. B., & Roland, S. B. (2007). Here come the Millennials, ready or not! In *Generations at school: Building an age-friendly learning community* (pp. 1–11). New York: Corwin.

Newmann, F. M. (2006). Improving achievement for all students: The meaning of staff-shared understanding and commitment. In W. D. Hawley & D. L. Rollie (Eds.), *The keys to effective schools: Educational reform as continuous improvement* (pp. 33–49). New York: Corwin.

Ramsey, R. D. (2007). *Don't teach the canaries not to sing: Creating a school culture that boosts achievement.* New York: Corwin.

Walter-Thomas, C., & DiPaola, M. F. (2003). What instructional leaders need to know about special education. In W. A. Owings & L. S. Kaplan (Eds.), *Best practices, best thinking, and emerging issues in school leadership* (pp. 125–136). New York: Corwin.

CHAPTER 4: COMMUNICATION ASPECTS OF GENERATION Y TEACHERS

Allen, M., Preiss, R., Gayle, B., & Burrell, N. (2002). *Interpersonal communication research.* Mahwah, NJ: Lawrence Erlbaum Associates.

November, A. (2003). Using technology to change school learning culture. In W. A. Owings & L. S. Kaplan (Eds.), *Best practices, best thinking, and emerging issues in school leadership* (pp. 95–101). New York: Corwin.

Olsen, G., & Fuller, M. L. (2003). Parent-teacher communication: Who's talking? In *Home-school relations: Working successfully with parents and families* (pp. 11–133). Boston: Pearson.

Richardson, W. (2006). *Blogs, wikis, podcasts, and other powerful web tools for classrooms.* New York: Corwin.

Roberts, D. F., & Foehr, U. G. (2008). Trends in media use. *The Future of Children, 18* (1), 11–37.

Schumaker, D. R., & Sommers, W. A. (2001). Communication—The foundation skill. In *Being a successful principal: Riding the wave of change without drowning* (pp. 1–22). Thousand Oaks, CA: Corwin.

Wyatt, R. L. III, & White, J. E. (2002). Making parent communication work. In *Making your first year a success* (pp. 95–106). Thousand Oaks, CA: Corwin.

Yan, J. (2008). Social technology as a new medium in the classroom. *New England Journal of Higher Education, 22* (4), 27, 29–30.

Zheng, R., Perez, J., Williamson, J., & Flygare, J. (2008). WebQuests as perceived by teachers: Implications for online teaching and learning. *Journal of Computer Assisted Learning, 24,* 295–304.

CHAPTER 5: HIRING AND COMPENSATION FOR GENERATION Y TEACHERS AND ADMINISTRATORS

Garvey, C. (2005). Philosophizing compensation. *HRMagazine, 50* (1), 73–78.

Grensing-Pophas, L. (2005). Health education turns proactive. *HRMagazine, 50* (4), 101–104.

Joiner, L. L. (2002). Life-saving lessons: What have schools learned since Columbine about keeping students safe? *American School Board Journal, 189* (3), 14–18.

Maurer, S. D. (2002). A practitioner-based analysis of interviewer job expertise and scale format as contextual factors in situational interviews. *Personnel Psychology, 55* (2), 267–306.

Posthuma, R. A., Morgeson, F. P., & Campion, M. A. (2002). Beyond employment interview validity: A comprehensive narrative review of recent research and trends over time. *Personnel Psychology, 55* (1), 1–81.

Progressive Policy Institute. (2002). *Better pay for better teaching—Making teacher compensation pay off in the age of accountability.* Washington, DC: The Institute.

Stites, J. (2005). Equal pay for the sexes. *HRMagazine, 50* (5), 64–69.

CHAPTER 6: RETAINING GENERATION Y THROUGH ASSESSMENT AND PROFESSIONAL GROWTH

Cederblom, D., & Pemerl, D. E. (2002). From performance appraisal to performance management: One agency's experience. *Public Personnel Management, 31* (2), 131–140.

Coppola, A. J., Scricca, D. B., & Connors, G. E. (2004). *Supportive supervision: Becoming a teacher of teachers.* (A joint publication with the National Association of Secondary School Principals.) Thousand Oaks, CA: Corwin.

Danielson, C., & McGreal, T. L. (2000). *Teacher evaluation: To enhance professional practice.* Princeton, NJ: Educational Testing Service.

DuFour, R. (2004). What is a professional learning community? *Educational Leadership, 61* (8), 6–11.

Glickman, C. D., Gordon, S. P., & Ross-Gordon, J. M. (2004). *SuperVision and instructional leadership: A developmental approach* (6th ed.). Boston: Allyn & Bacon.

Kelley, C., Heneman, H. III, & Milanowski, A. (2002). Teacher motivation and school-based performance awards. *Educational Administration Quarterly, 38* (3), 372–401.

Margulus, L. S., & Melin, J. A. (2004). *Performance appraisals made easy: Tools for evaluating teachers and support staff.* Thousand Oaks, CA: Corwin.

Peterson, K. (2002). The professional development of principals: Innovations and opportunities. *Educational Administration Quarterly, 38* (2), 213–232.

Senge, P., Cambron-McCabe, N., Lucas, T., Smith, B., Dutton, J., & Kleiner, A. (2000). *Schools that learn: A fifth discipline fieldbook for educators, parents, and everyone who cares about education.* New York: Doubleday.

Sullivan, S., & Glanz, J. (2004). *Supervision that improves teaching: Strategies and techniques* (2nd ed.). Thousand Oaks, CA: Corwin.

Wiles, J. W. (2004). *Supervision: A guide to practice* (6th ed.). Upper Saddle River, NJ: Merrill/Prentice Hall.

Index

CORWIN

A SAGE Company

The Corwin logo—a raven striding across an open book—represents the union of courage and learning. Corwin is committed to improving education for all learners by publishing books and other professional development resources for those serving the field of PreK–12 education. By providing practical, hands-on materials, Corwin continues to carry out the promise of its motto: **"Helping Educators Do Their Work Better."**